Beaver Valley Ontario in Photos,
Saving Our History
One Photo at a Time

Photography
by Barbara Raué
2013

Series Name:
Cruising Ontario

Book 27: Beaver Valley

Cover photo: Home in Flesherton

Series Name: Cruising Ontario

Book 1: London
Book 2: Dundas
Book 3: Hamilton
Book 4: Oakville
Book 5: Chesley
Book 6: Stoney Creek
Book 7: Waterdown
Book 8: Owen Sound
Book 9: Mount Forest
Book 10: Dundalk
Book 11: Burford and Area
Book 12: Waterford and Area
Book 13: Drumbo and Area
Book 14: Sheffield and Area
Book 15: Tavistock and Area
Book 16: Ancaster and Mount Hope
Book 17: Innerkip
Book 18: Brantford
Book 19: Burlington
Book 20: Guelph and Area
Book 21: Ayr
Book 22: Erin
Book 23: Goderich
Book 24: Lucknow
Book 25: Orangeville and Area
Book 26: Toronto
Book 27: Beaver Valley
Book 28: Collingwood
Book 29: Peterborough and Area

Other Books by Barbara Raue

Coins of Gold

Arrows, Indians and Love

The Life and Times of Barbara
Volume 1: Inventions That Have Enhanced My Life
Volume 2: Entertainment That I Have Enjoyed
Volume 3: East Coast Trips
Volume 4: Olympics
Volume 5: Wonders of the World
Volume 6: Caribbean Cruises
Volume 7: Animals
Volume 8: Storms
Volume 9: Wars

Beaver Valley

The Beaver Valley is located in southern Ontario at the southern tip of Georgian Bay. The Beaver River flows north through the valley emptying into Georgian Bay in the town of Thornbury. It is a productive agricultural area producing 25% of Ontario's apple crop on 7,500 acres of apple orcchards. The main towns in the valley from Flesherton at the south end are Kimberley and Thornbury. Grey Road 13 follows the meandering Beaver River along the valley floor. It rises briefly before crossing the river again at Heathcote.

Clarksburg

Clarksburg, the hidden gateway between the picturesque backroads of the Beaver Valley, the slopes of the Blue Mountains, and the shores of Georgian Bay, is located just south of Thornbury on Grey Road 13. The Beaver River cascades through a series of picturesque rapids from Clendenan Dam through the village and north to Georgian Bay. In 1858 William Jabez Marsh travelled from Holland Landing to purchase 500 acres of Crown land adjacent to the village of Thornbury. After choosing a location for his own farm, he donated 2.5 acres for the building of a church and rectory. The first church was a frame building erected in 1863 and named St. George's and was located in the newly established village of Clarksburg immediately adjacent to the border with Thornbury in order to serve both municipalities. The original church served until 1899 when it was replaced by the present brick structure erected on the same site. Once the brick church was completed, the original frame building was dismantled and transported in mid-winter by horse-drawn sleighs to Beaverdale where it was reassembled and continued to serve the congregation there for another 50 years.

The brick rectory next to the church was built in 1867 and has been well maintained

Markdale

Markdale is located on Highway 10 north of Flesherton. Settlement began in 1849, and it was incorporated as a village in 1888 with a thriving business centre, three churches, a bank, a school, a wagon shop and a drug store. The beautiful Beaver Valley lies just a few miles to the east of Markdale.

Craigleith

Craigleith is located east of Thornbury on Georgian Bay. The name is Gaelic meaning rocky bay and the town was given the name by Andrew Craig Fleming, one of the community's earliest settlers. Craigleith was the home of Sir Sandford Fleming who contributed to the establishment of standard time earning him the title of "The Father of Standard Time." Fleming also designed the first Canadian postage stamp; issued in 1851, it cost three pennies and depicted the beaver, now the national animal of Canada. The Sanford family began operating a quarry and lumber mill in Craigleith which provided essential building materials to their new settlement.

On November 24, 1872 the steamer "Mary Ward" ran aground two kilometers offshore as she was travelling from Sarnia to Collingwood. A group of local fishermen rescued those remaining on board; however, the last of three rescue boats capsized and eight passengers drowned.

One of the last remaining wooden CNR stations is located here.

Flesherton

Flesherton is located at the junction of Highway 10 and Grey County Road 4. In 1850, 25-year-old William Kingston Flesher surveyed a portion of the Township of Artemesia. The north-south Toronto-Sydenham Road and east-west Durham Road which both ran through the township, were built shortly after the survey was finished, thereby opening the area to settlement. The intersection of the two roads which lay in a small valley was named Artemesia Corners. As was usual for the time, Flesher was paid for his work in property within the survey area. He chose the valley containing Artemesia Corners and laid out a portion in village lots. Aaron Munshaw arrived as the first settler and built a tavern on the southeast corner of the intersection of the two roads. In 1864 as the village grew, Munshaw built a larger inn and stagecoach stop that incorporated some parts of the original hotel. This building, operated as a hotel by the Munshaw family until the 1960s, is now known as Munshaw House and still stands on the original spot.

Throughout the 1850s many Scottish immigrants arrived to claim lots and began to clear the land. Mr. Flesher continued to develop the valley economy building a sawmill and a grist mill on the Boyne River that flowed through the bottom of the valley. He encouraged other businesses to settle in the area. In his honour, the name of the settlement was changed to Flesherton.

The red brick Methodist Church was built in 1877. In 1879 Chalmers Presbyterian Church was built where the Toronto-Sydenham Road crossed the Boyne River. In 1926 the Methodist Church joined with Chalmers Presbyterian to form St. John's United Church. The combined congregation chose to retain the highly visible Methodist building and sold the much smaller Presbyterian building.

Leith

Leith, located on the south shore of Georgian Bay, is nine kilometres northeast of the city of Owen Sound. It is the boyhood home of the renowned Canadian landscape artist Tom Thomson who is buried in the pioneer cemetery behind Leith United Church.

Heathcote

Heathcote is located in Grey County on the Beaver Road and Concession Road 13 south of Thornbury. William Fleming settled here in the 1840s and for a time the place was called Williamstown after him. That name was already in use elsewhere in Ontario, so when the post office opened in 1859, this community was called Heathcote, possibly after a place of that name in Derbyshire, England.

Meaford

Meaford is located on the southern shore of Georgian Bay, on Highway 26 between Thornbury and Owen Sound. In 1837 inhabitants of St. Vincent Township petitioned the government requesting that land at the mouth of the Bighead River be reserved as a landing place. In 1841 there was a saw mill, a grist mill, several roads had been constructed to the landing place, and a post office was established. The town plot of Meaford was laid out in 1845.

Meaford Town Hall was built in 1908-09 with Palladian lines and stately Doric columns after the original building built in 1864 had become dilapidated and was destroyed by fire on October 5, 1907. Local contractor James Sparling recycled as much of the original town hall's brick as possible in the construction of the new building. Like many public buildings across small-town Ontario, Meaford Hall was made to be more than a town hall. The building housed the council chambers and town offices. The chambers also served as a court room and there were two tiny jail cells in the basement. At the other end of the building was the Meaford Public Library. Farmers used the basement on market day, and the space has been used for a ballroom, meeting area, and Boy Scouts hall. It has housed the Women's Institute, the Meaford Quilters, a Senior Citizens' Club, and the Senior Men's Euchre club. The second floor Opera House was the cultural heart of the community. Local plays, high school graduations, concerts and famous speakers have all made use of the theatre. In 1967, the library moved to a bigger space in the old post office. The Meaford Police Department left the hall in 1996. The town vacated the old offices in 2002. In 2003, Meaford secured a grant to restore and renovate the building. Thousands of volunteer hours later, the Meaford Hall Arts and Cultural Centre opened for business in the spring of 2006.

The building housing the current museum was built in 1895 as the towns Pumping Station. The Public Utilities Department was later relocated to the Pump House and the building was called the "Power House." During the 1940s, the chimney was removed. Cyrus Sing, a local citizen, donated his collection of memorabilia to the Town, and the building which had been vacant for awhile was converted to a museum and opened to the public on July 1, 1961. Due to a continually expanding collection, several renovations and additions have been made to the building over the years.

Born in Nova Scotia, Margaret Marshall Saunders (1861-1947) was a novelist whose second book "Beautiful Joe" achieved international recognition. Inspired by a visit to Meaford in 1892, it is based on the story of a dog rescued from a brutal master by a local miller, William Moore. In 1994 the Beautiful Joe Heritage Society was formed to honour the life and story of Beautiful Joe and the literary and humane achievements of Margaret Saunders. Beautiful Joe Park is located in Meaford.

Thornbury

Thornbury is located on Georgian Bay between Meaford and Collingwood. The Township of Thornbury was incorporated in 1833. In 1855 the town's first business, a milling operation, was set up, followed by a general store, blacksmith, cooper and fanning mill shops, grist and saw mills, and a post office. In 1887, feeling they were unfairly burdened with high taxes, the businessmen of Thornbury petitioned for independence from the Town of Collingwood. After much negotiating, they received it and the Township of Thornbury became the Town of Thornbury. The apple packing industry took root in Thornbury in 1885. At the Thornbury Village Cidery, they produce Premium Apple Cider from apples grown in the area, cider that is light, crisp and refreshing.

On January 1, 2001, the Town of Thornbury and the small settlements in the Township of Collingwood were amalgamated. Thornbury is the primary population centre. The town's territory includes the communities of Banks, Camperdown, Castle Glen Estates, Christie Beach, Clarksburg, Craigleith, Duncan, Gibraltar, Heathcote, Kolapore, Little Germany, Lora Bay, Loree, Ravenna, Red Wing, Slabtown and Victoria Corners.

Victoria Corners

Victoria Corners is located on 21st Sideroad near Loree Forest and north of the hamlet of Banks.

Walter's Falls

Walter's Falls is located south of Owen Sound on Grey County Road 29. It was the site of a saw mill and woollen mill. The saw mill burned down but the woollen mill remains. Water from Walter's Creek flows to form Walter's Falls.

Clarksburg

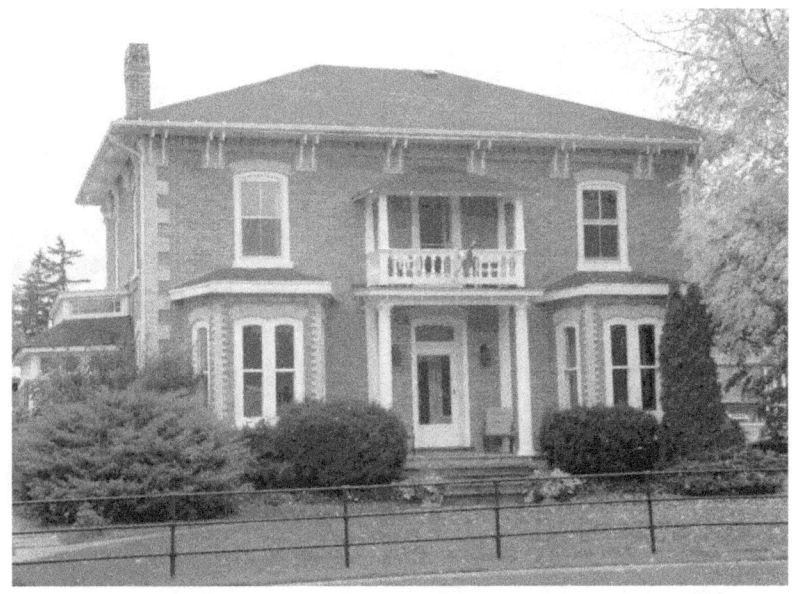

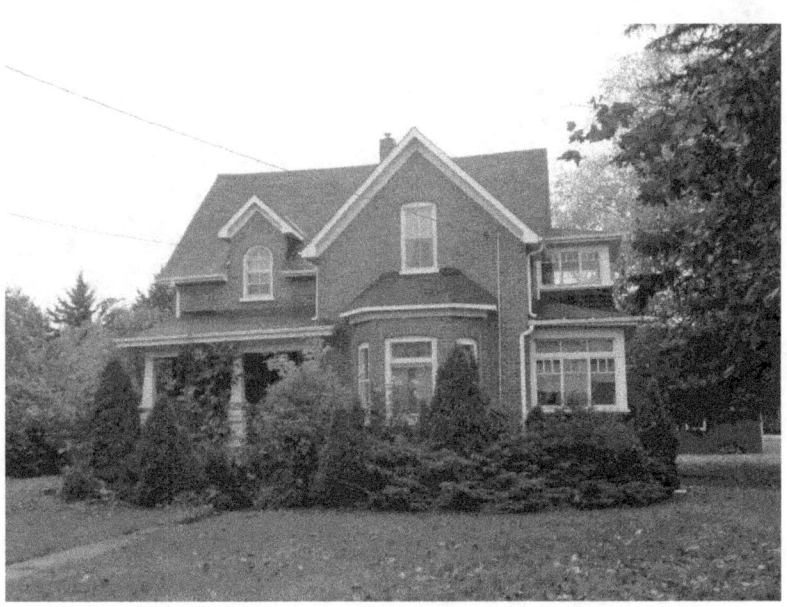

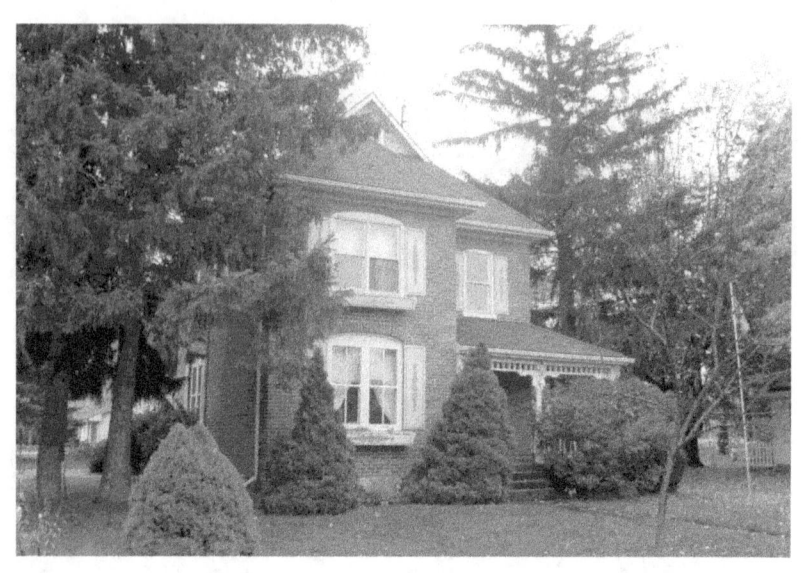

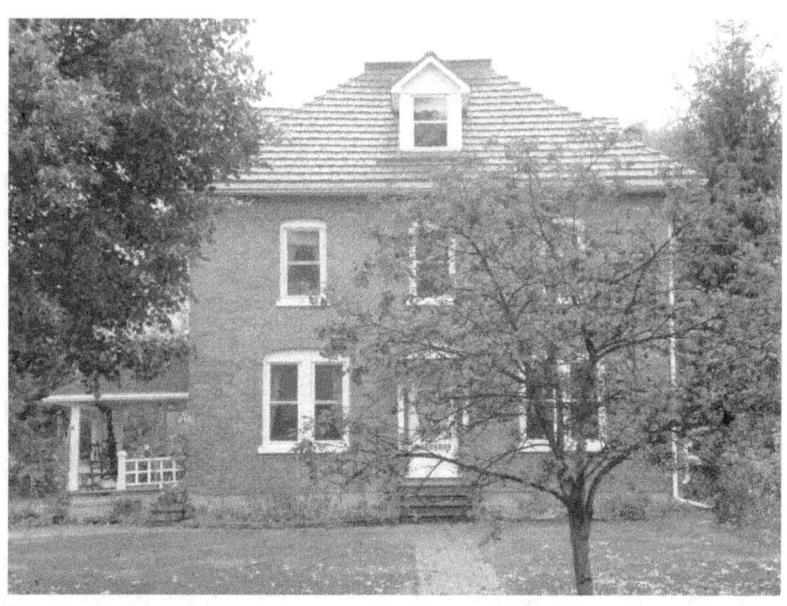

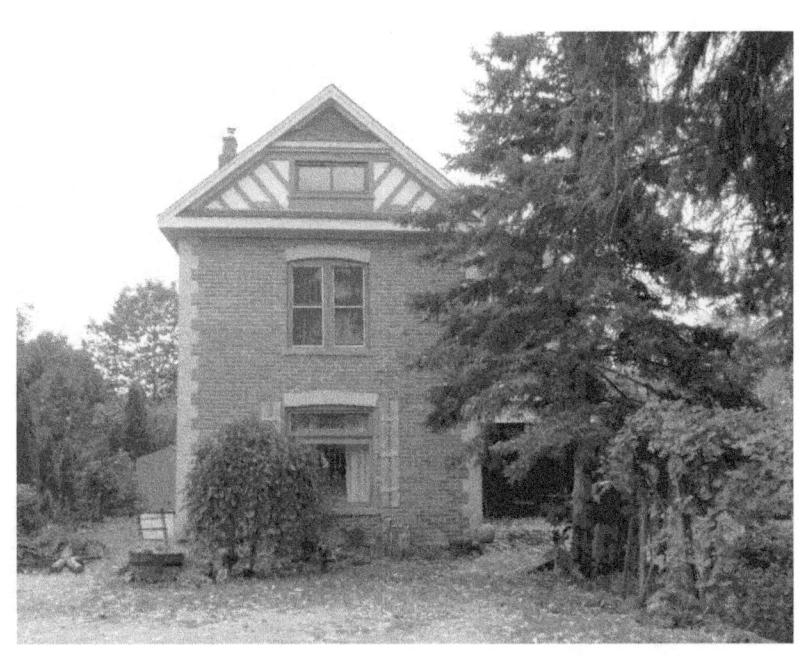

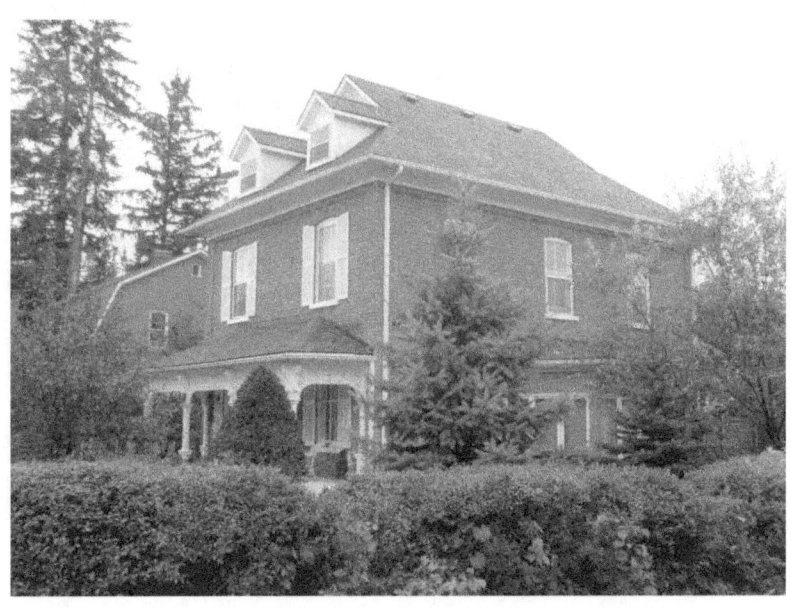

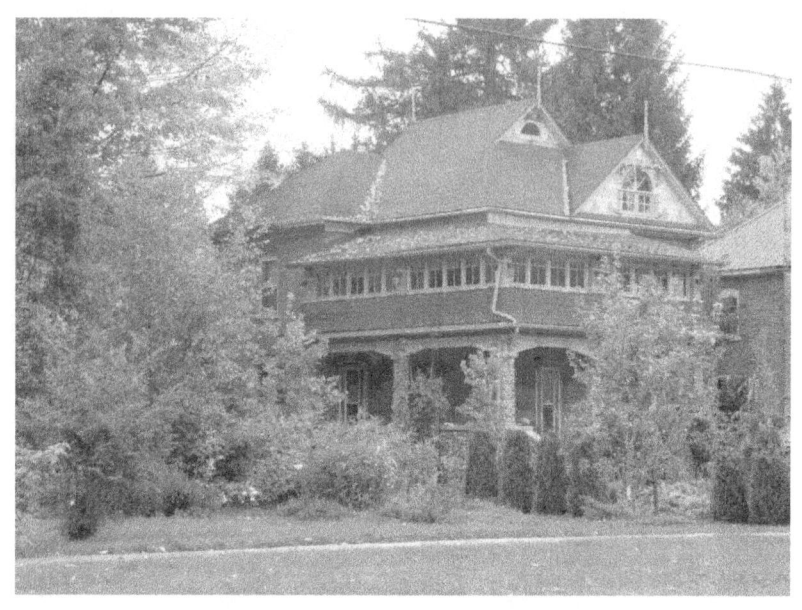

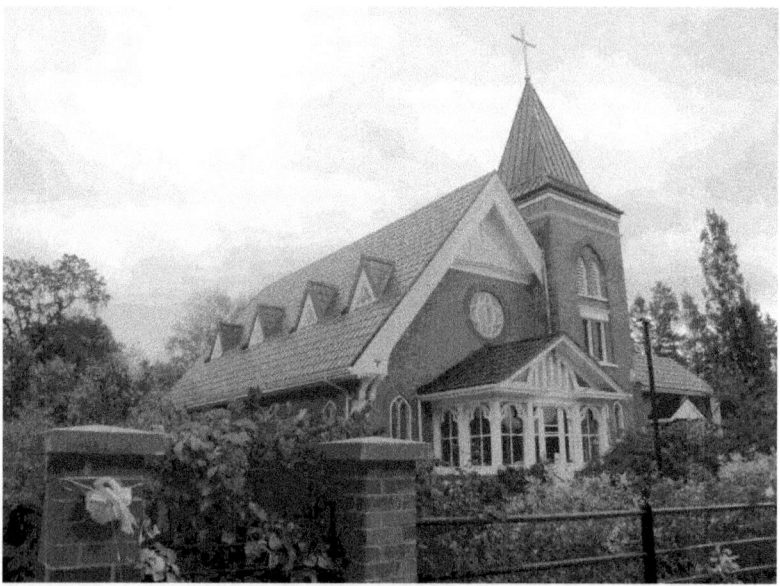

St. George's Anglican Church
166 Russell Street

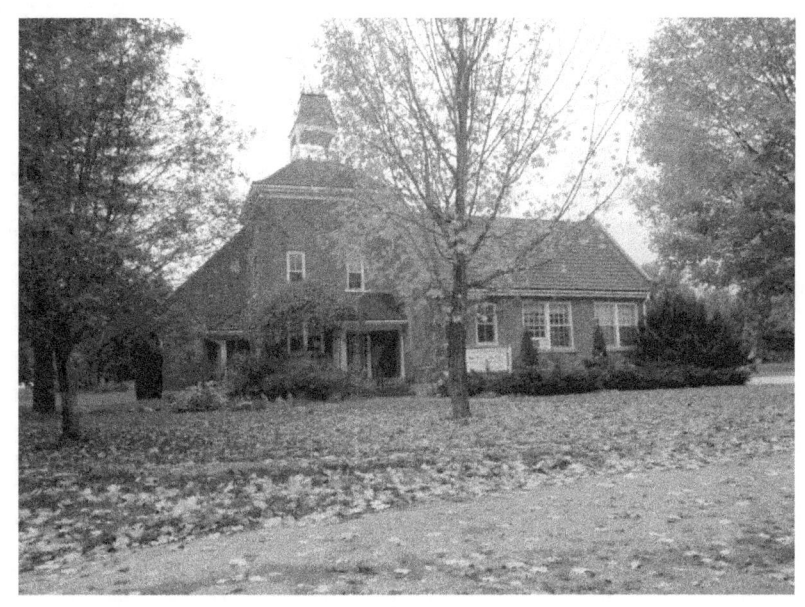

Markdale

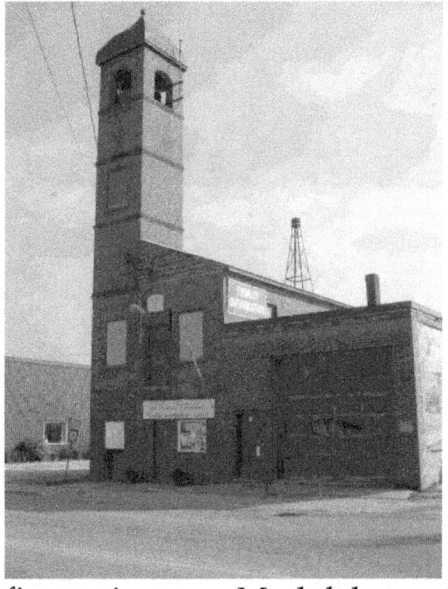

Historic fire station now Markdale tourist office

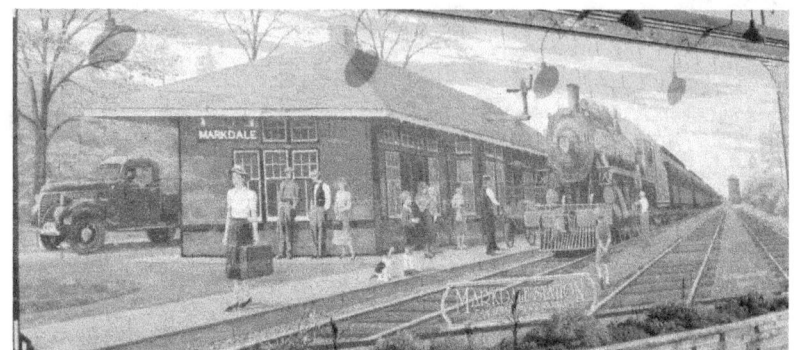

Mural of Markdale Station, Canadian Pacific Railway

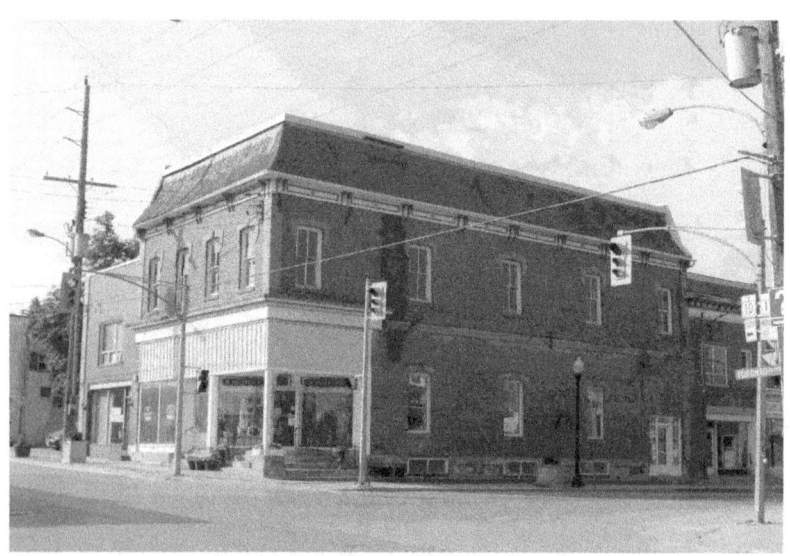

Corner of Toronto and Main Streets

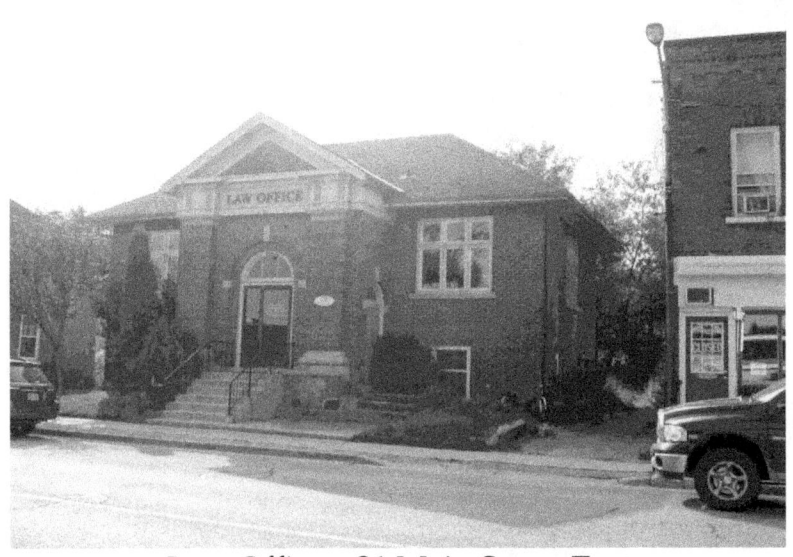

Law Office – 21 Main Street East

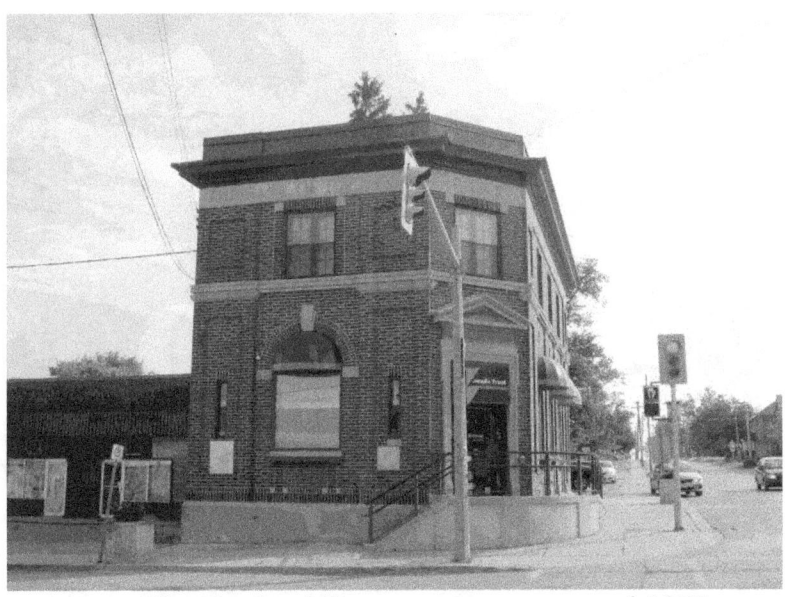

The Bank of Toronto, incorporated 1855

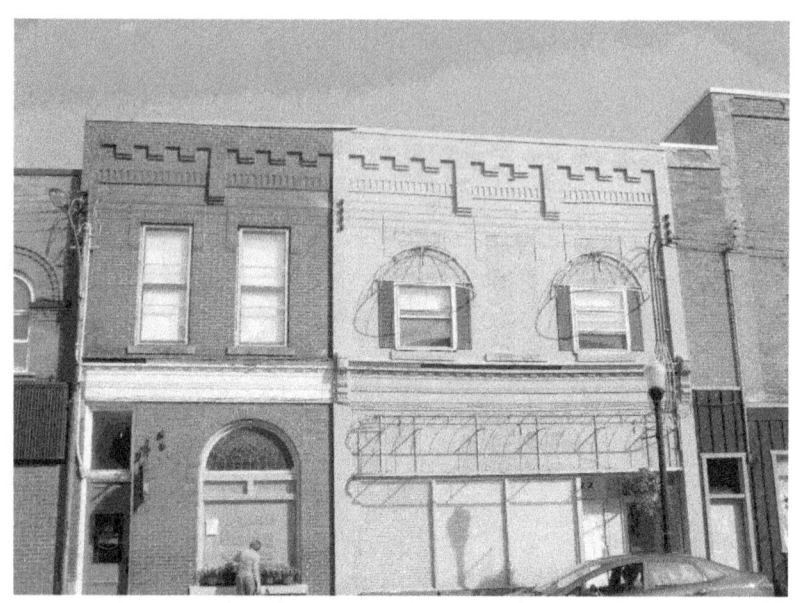

Downtown buildings

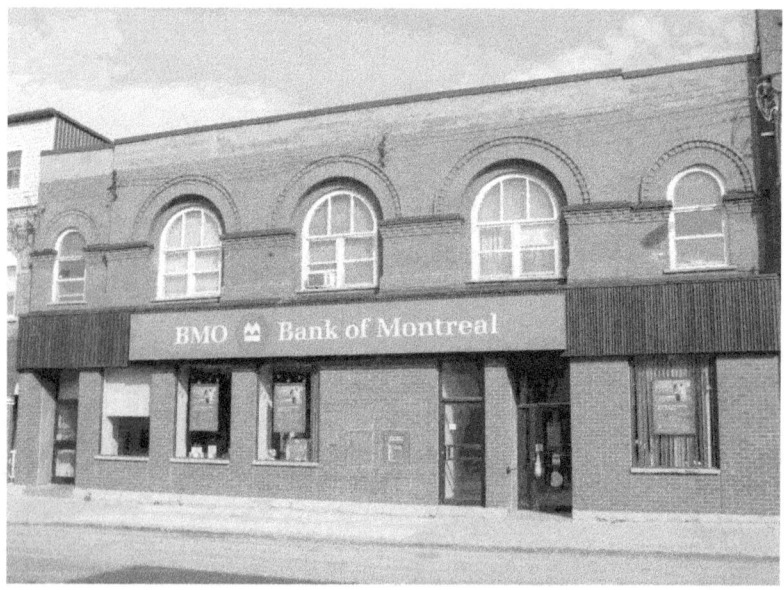

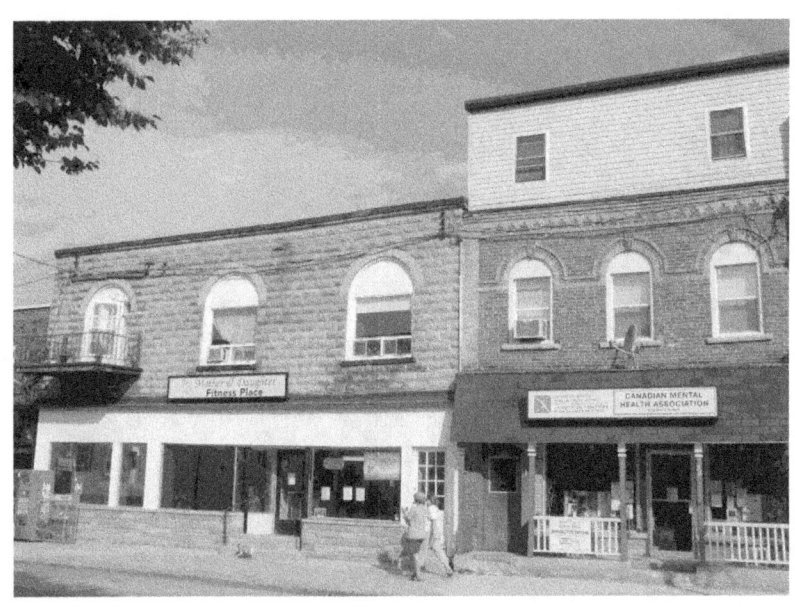

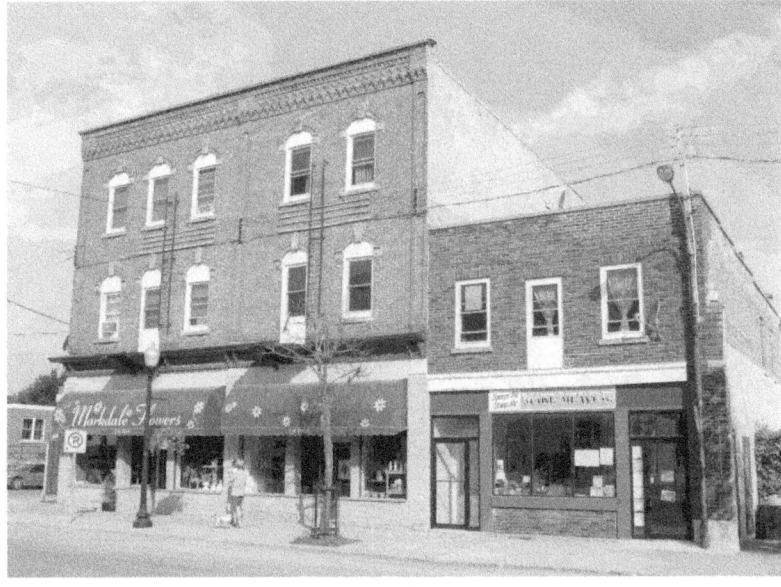

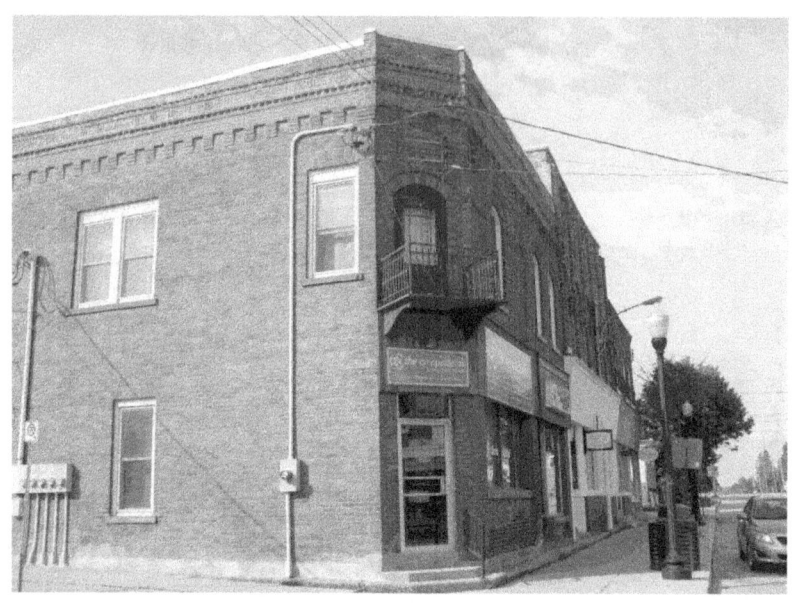

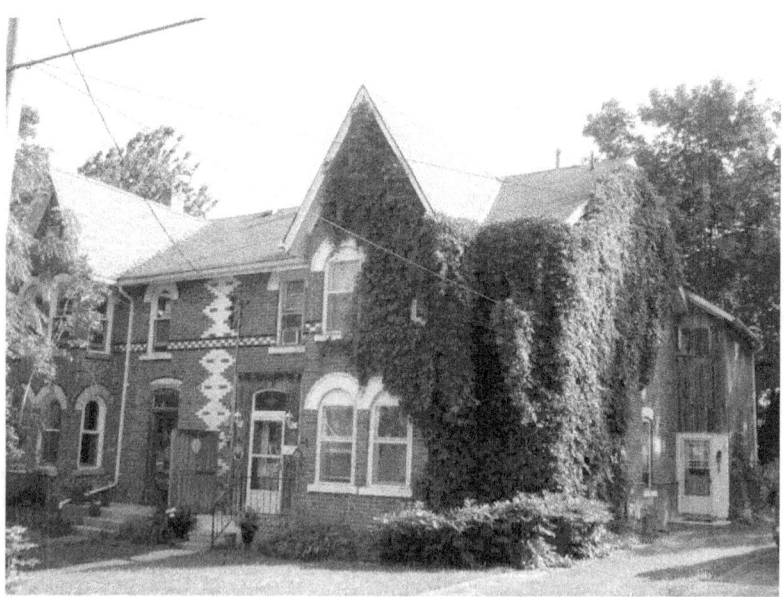

Red brick Gothic style house with white accents

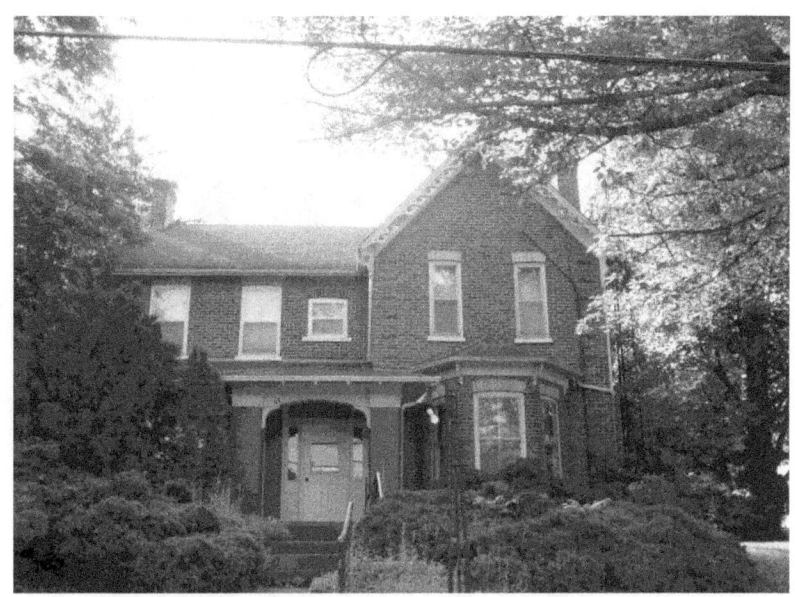

Note the gingerbread trim (bargeboard)

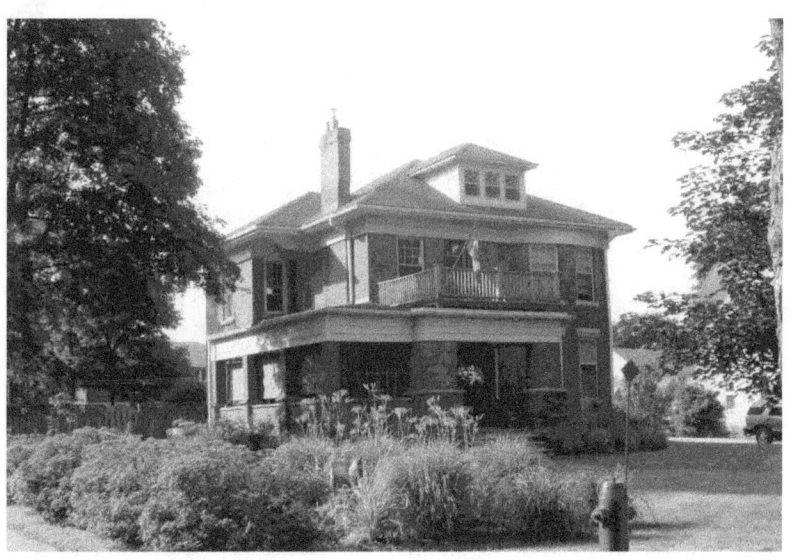

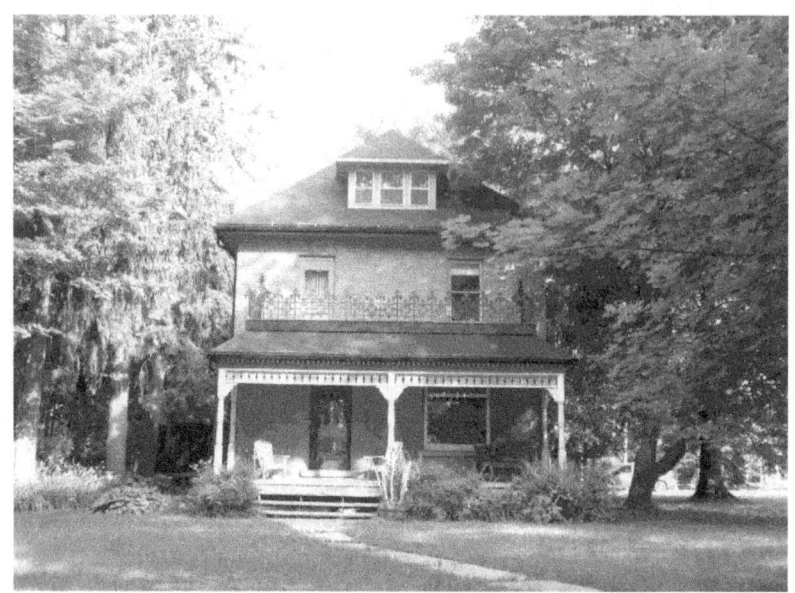

Beautiful iron crestwork above the veranda

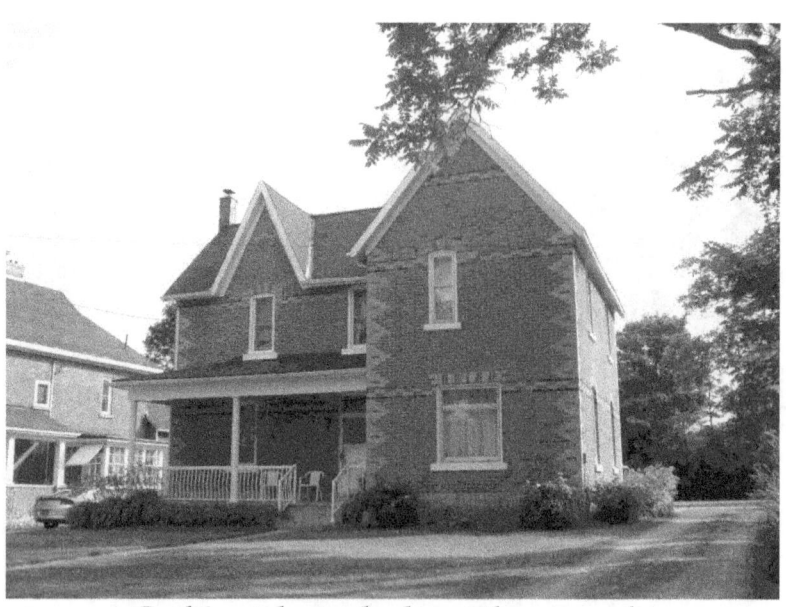

Gothic style peak above the veranda

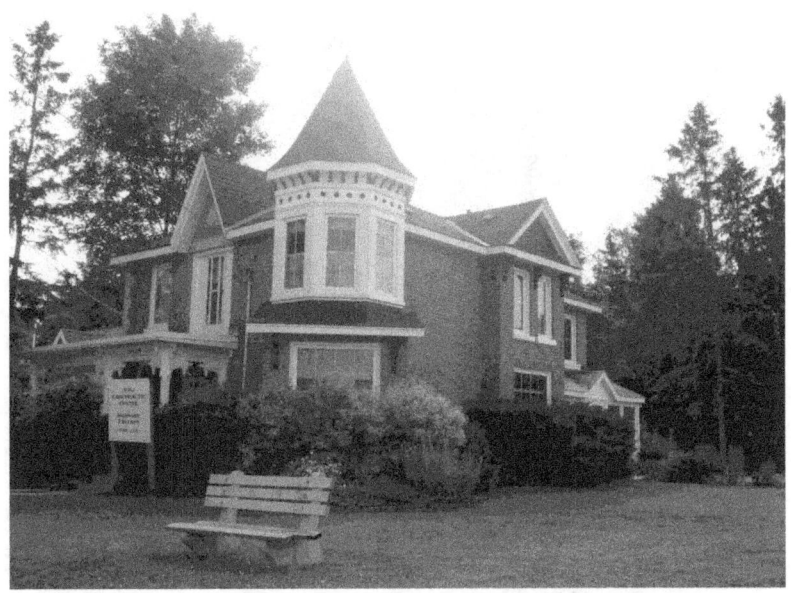

Beautiful round turret on the Gothic style home

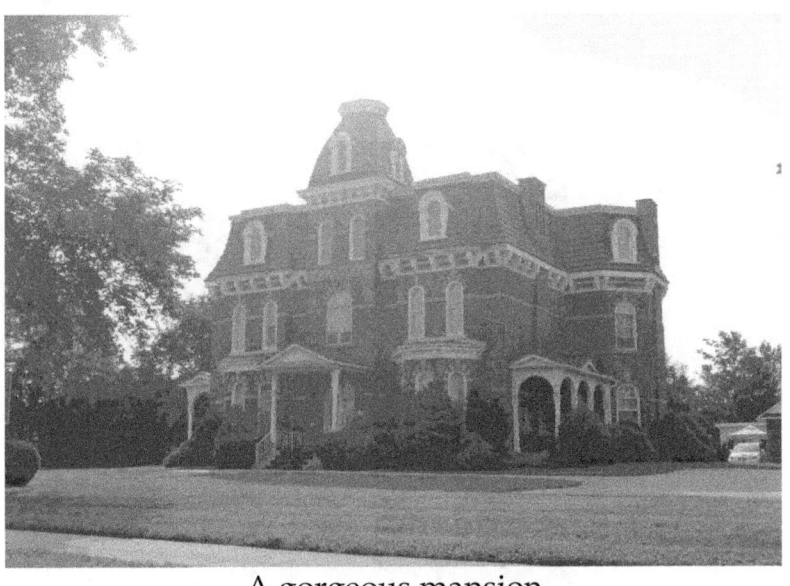

A gorgeous mansion

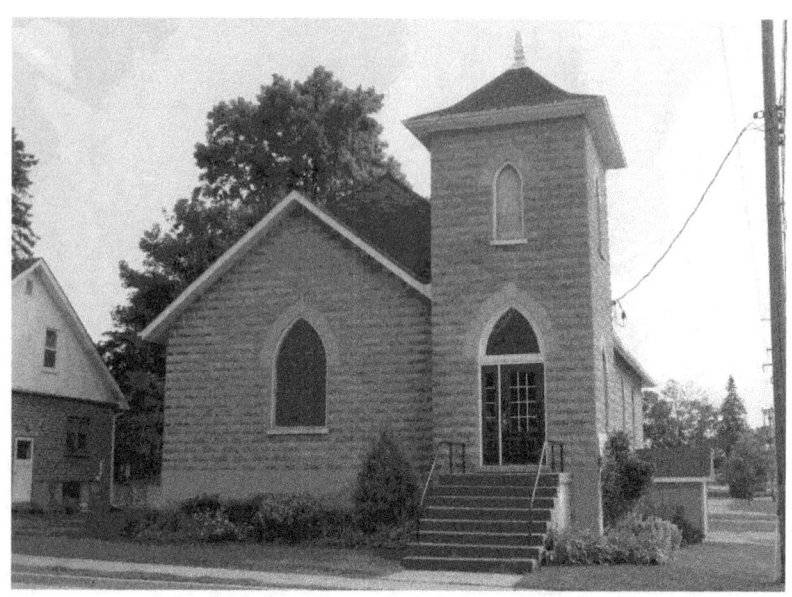

Markdale Church of the Nazarene

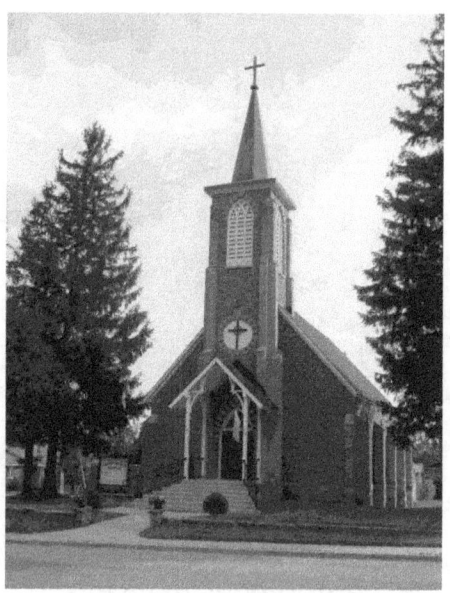

Christ Church Anglican

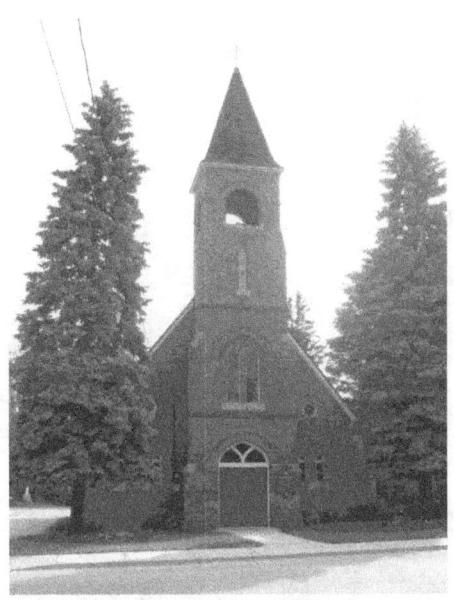

St. Joseph's Catholic Church

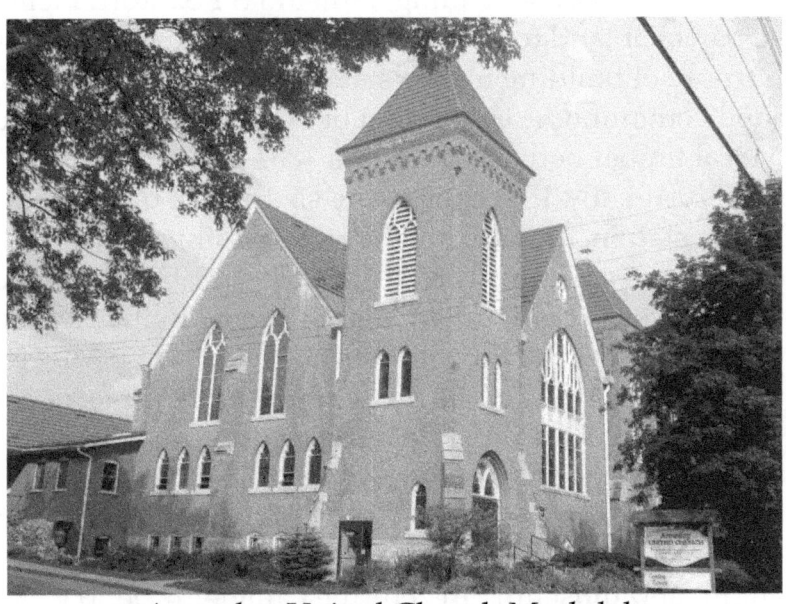

Annesley United Church Markdale

Craigleith

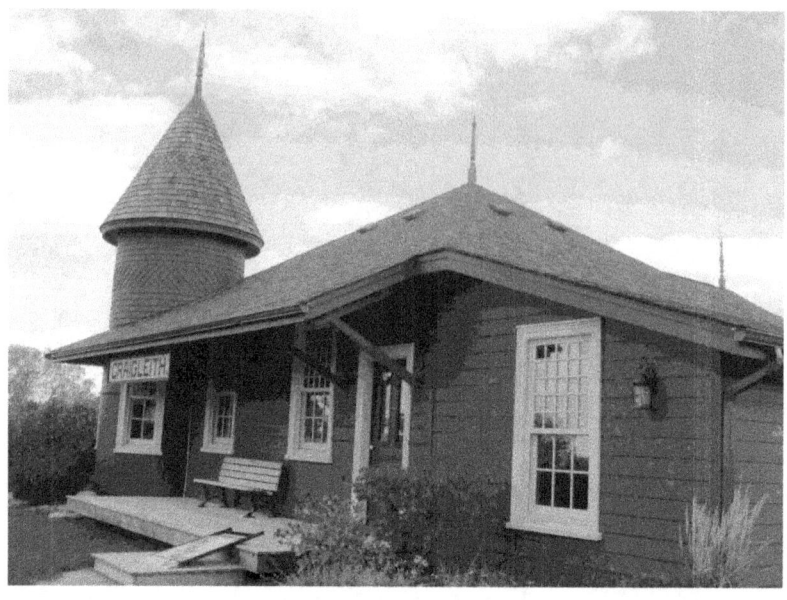

In 1872 Andrew Grieg Fleming, father of Sir Sanford Fleming, sold a parcel of land to the Northern Railway Company for the purpose of building a train station to serve his newly founded community. The station building was constructed from local timber between 1878 and 1881 and included a rounded turret. By 1881 there were six trains a day at the Craigleith station. In 1882, the Northern Railway was purchased by the Grand Trunk Railway. In 1923 the Grand Trunk became part of the Canadian National Railway. The convenience of the railway allowed businesses to be created and to prosper. In the 1940s the ski industry in Ontario began to grow with weekend ski trains from Toronto. Passenger service to the Craigleith station ended in 1960. In 1966 the station and lilac grove were saved from destruction by Kenn and Suyrea Knapman who re-opened the station as a restaurant and museum. In 2001 the Craigleith Depo was purchased by The Blue Mountains.

Flesherton

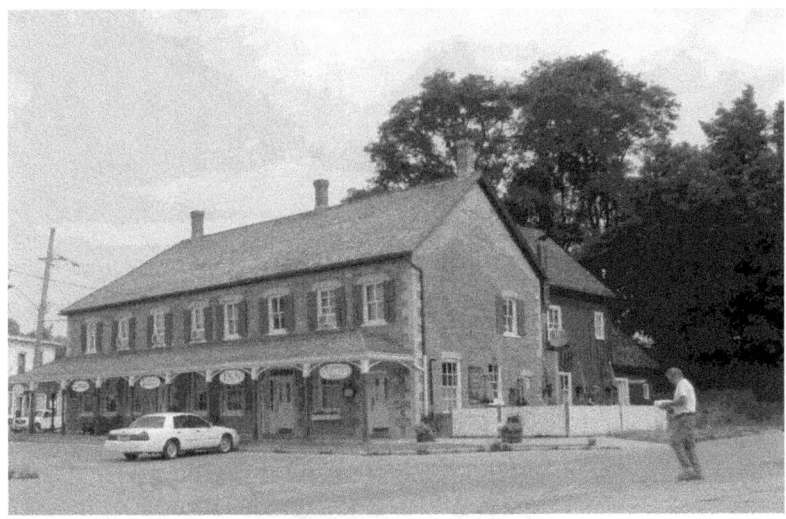

Munshawe House built in 1864 as a stagecoach stop at the junction of Toronto-Sydenham Road and Durham

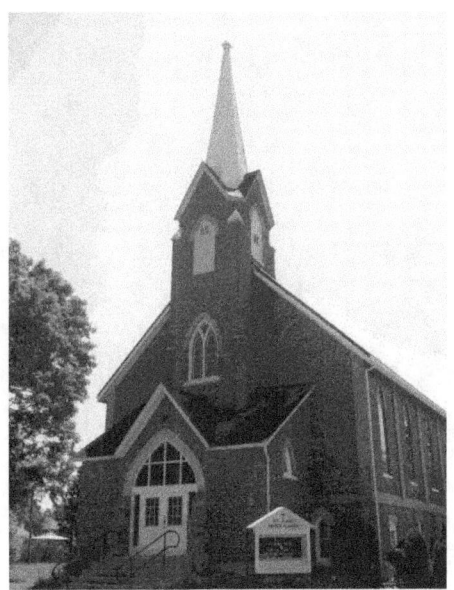

St. John's United Church – built in 1877 as the Methodist Church

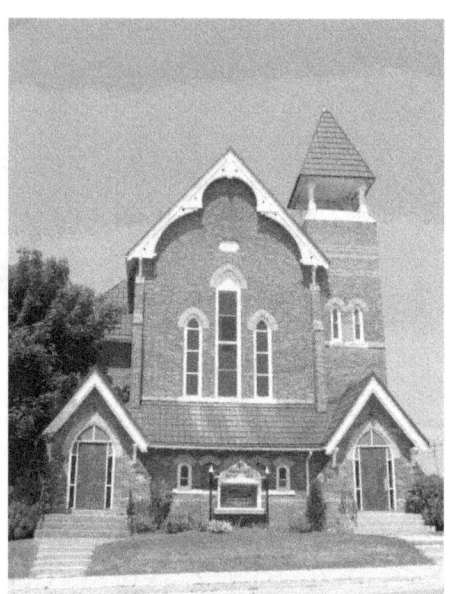

In 1886 Cedarside Baptist Church was built at the east end of the village.

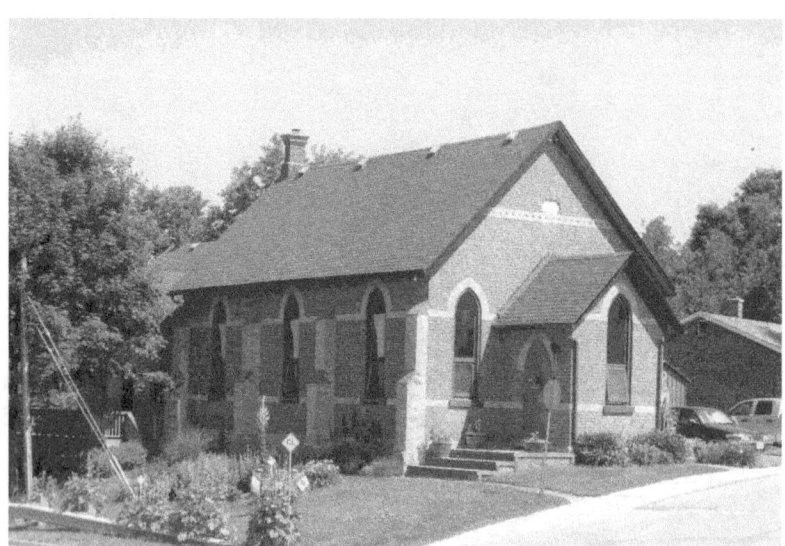

The former Chalmers Presbyterian Church built in 1879

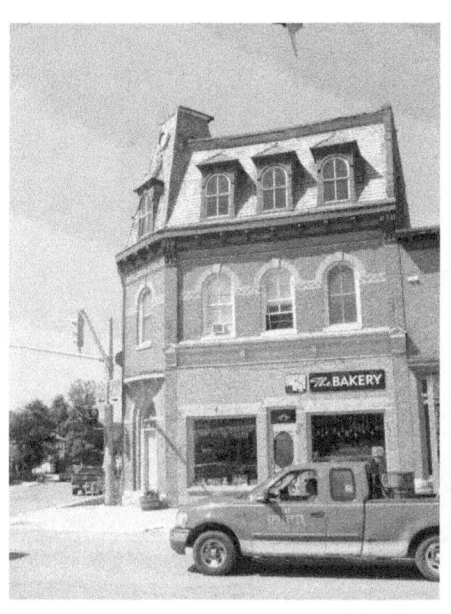

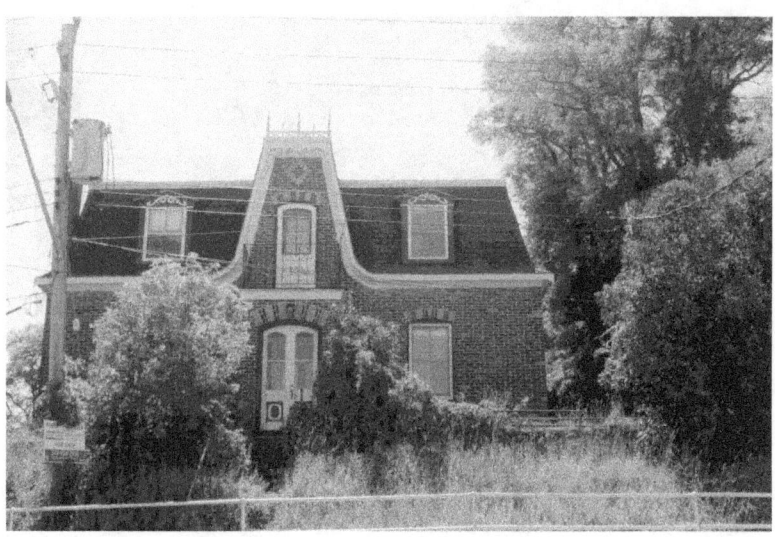

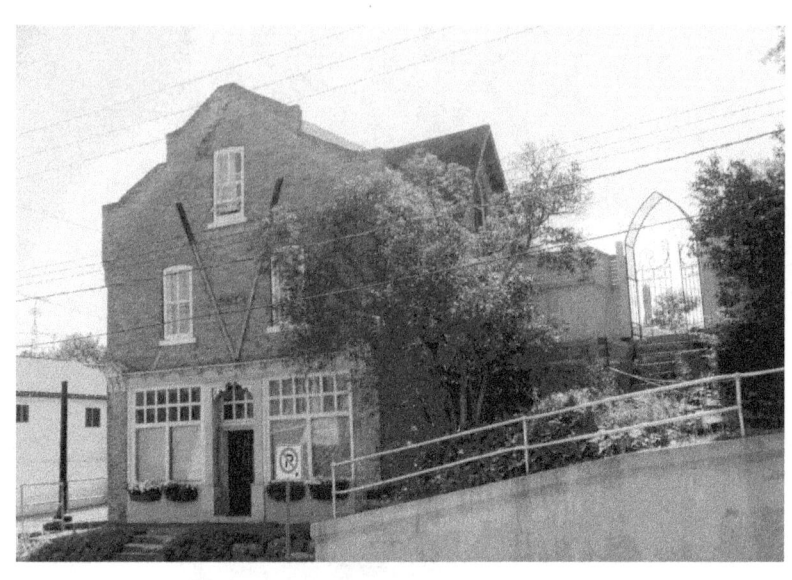

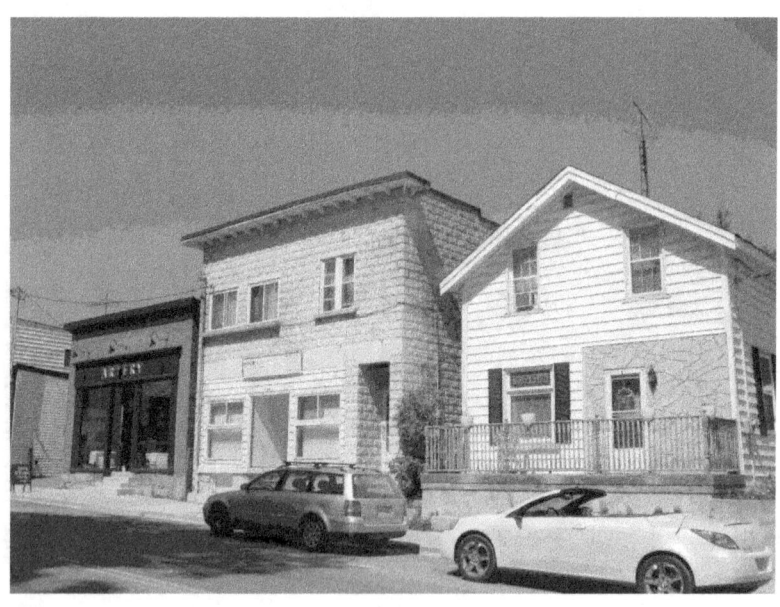

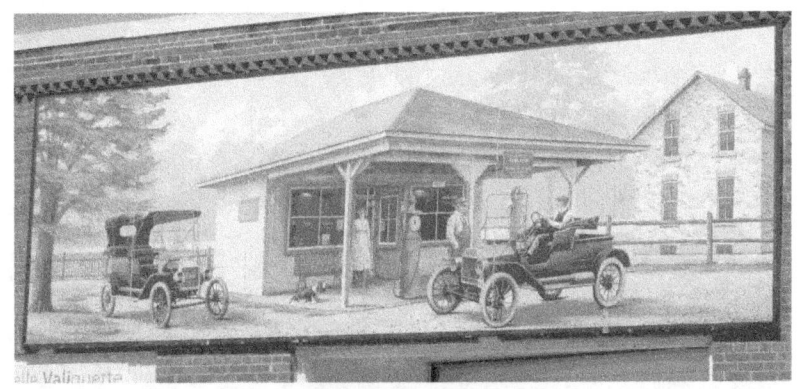

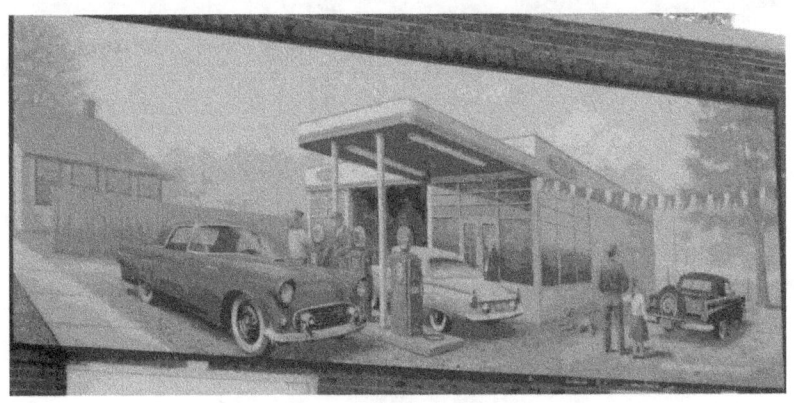

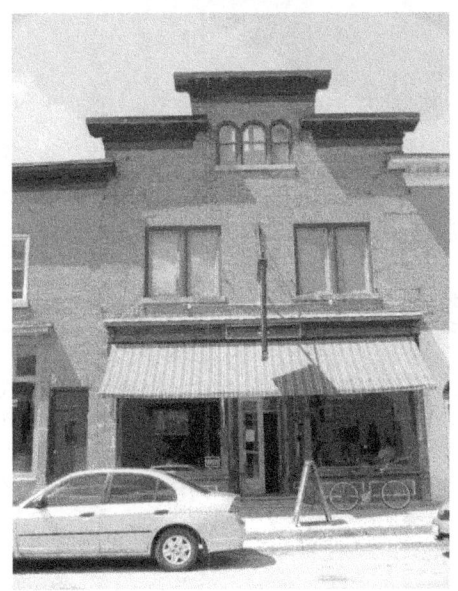

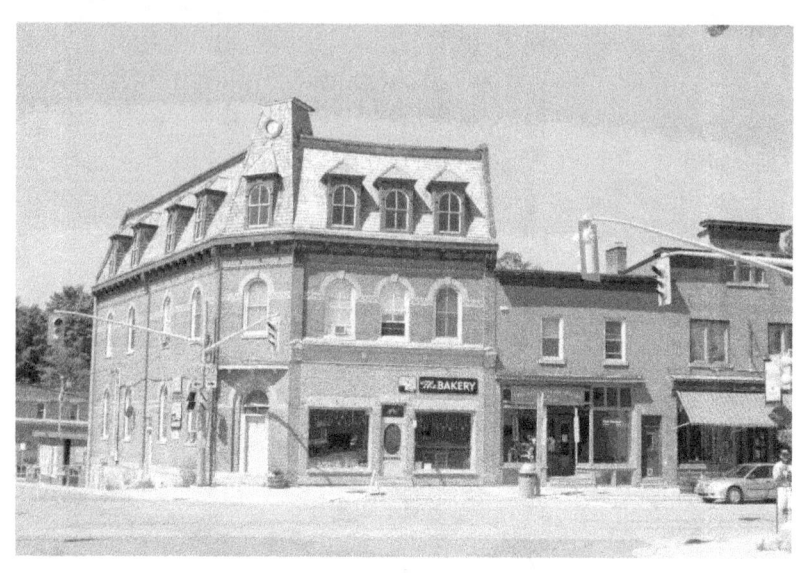

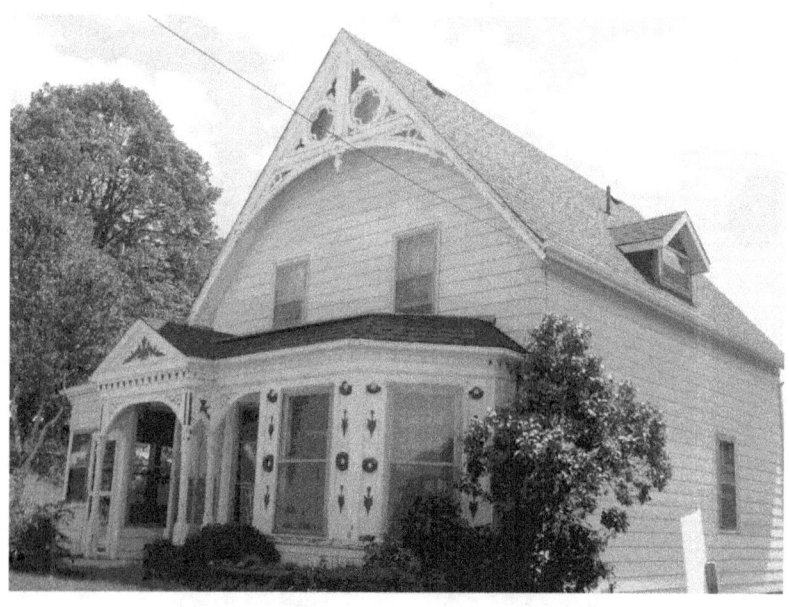

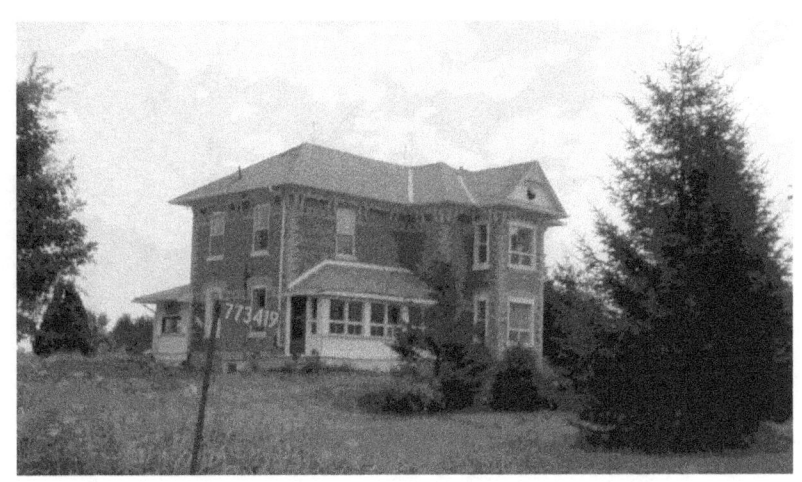

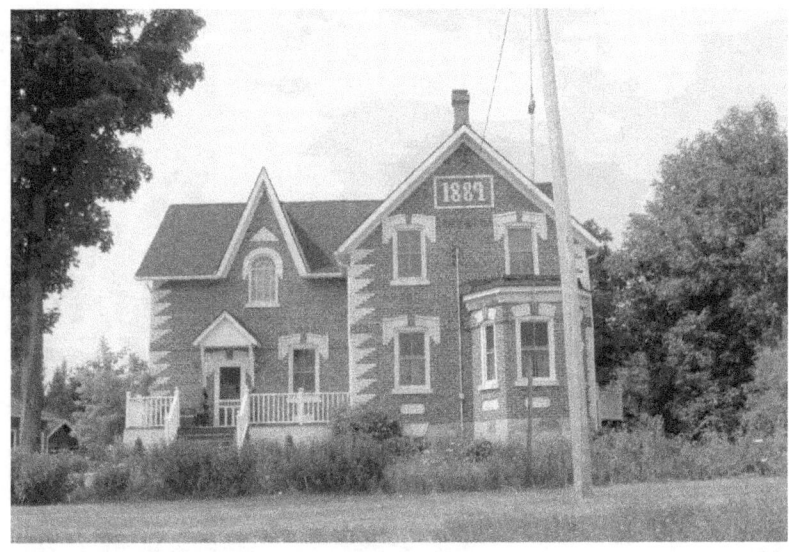

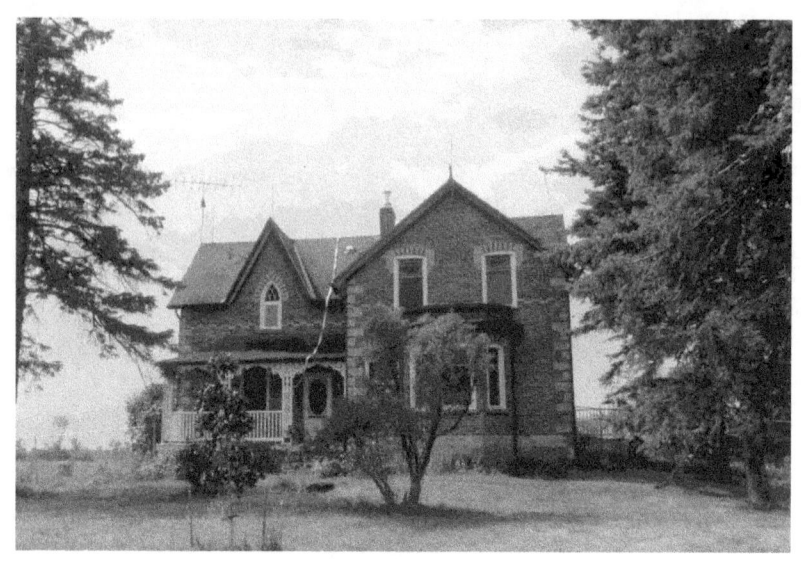

Leith

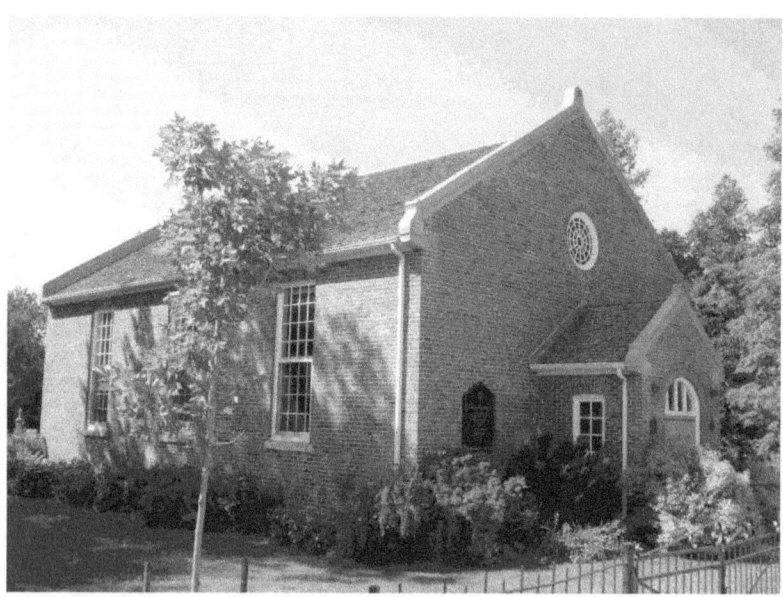

Leith United Church was erected in 1865 and closed in 1969. Since 1992 the church has been maintained by volunteers and is occasionally opened for special events.

Heathcote

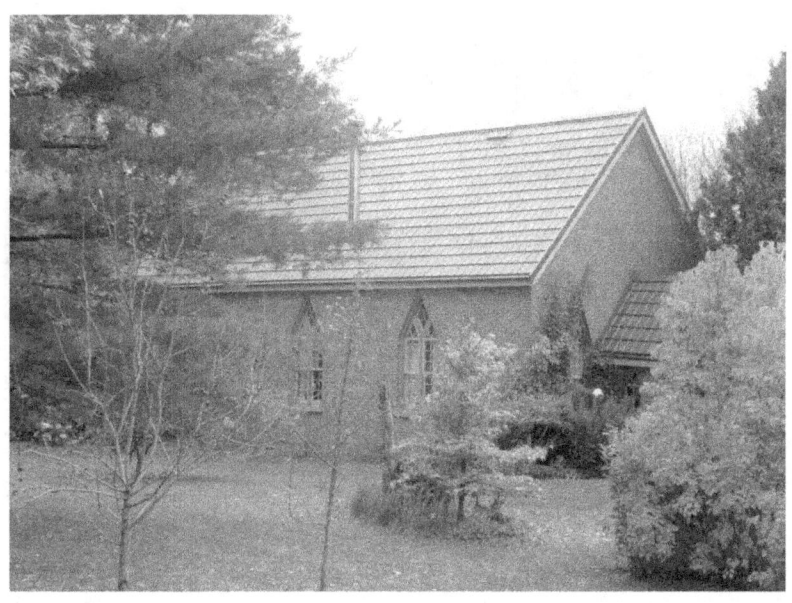

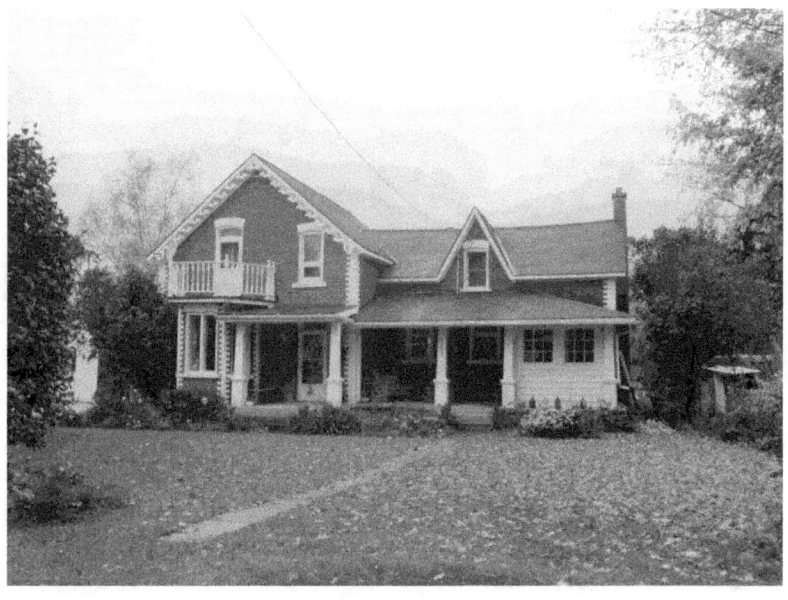

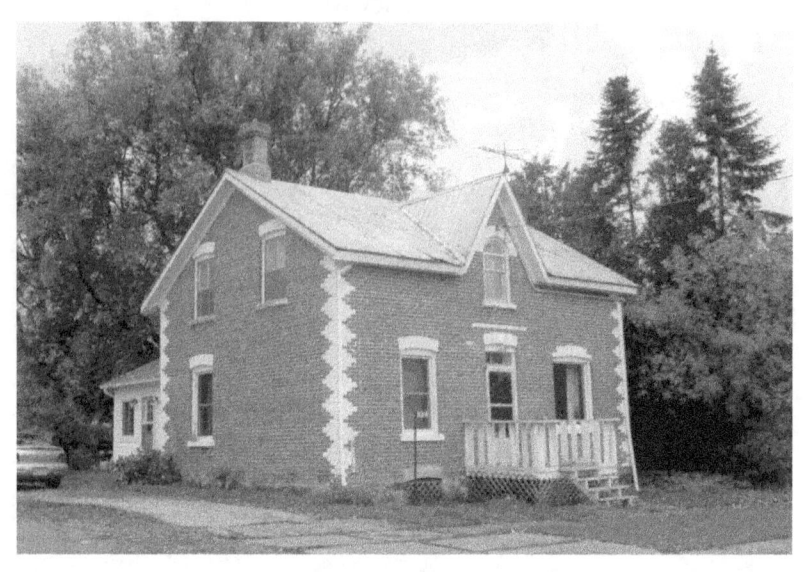

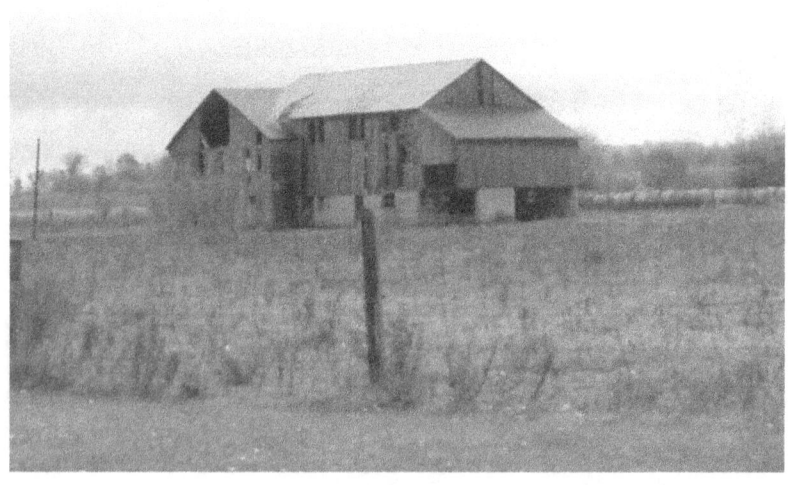

Meaford

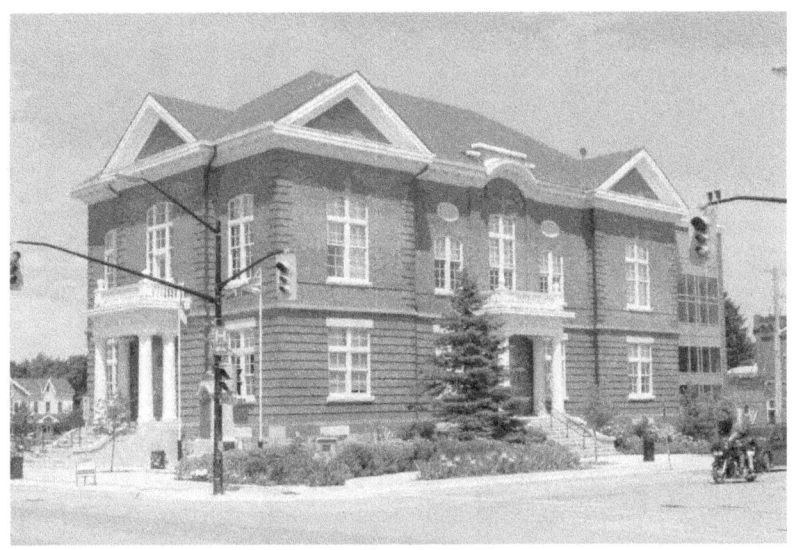

Meaford Hall

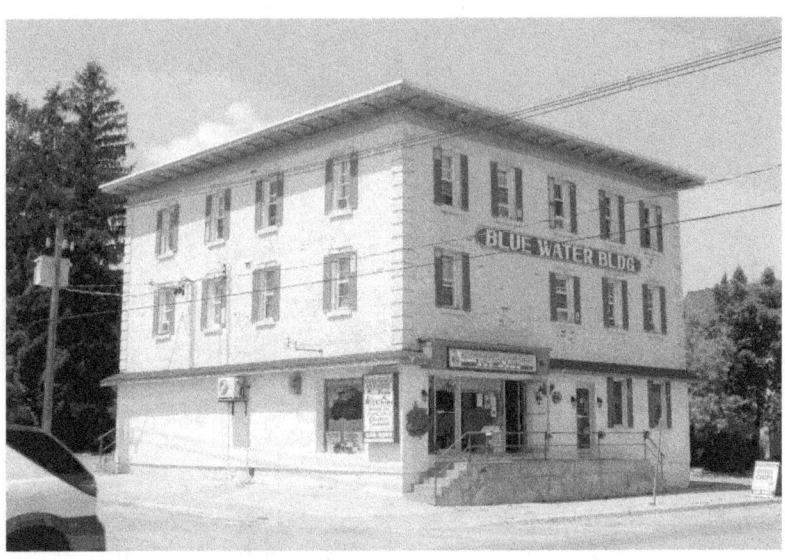

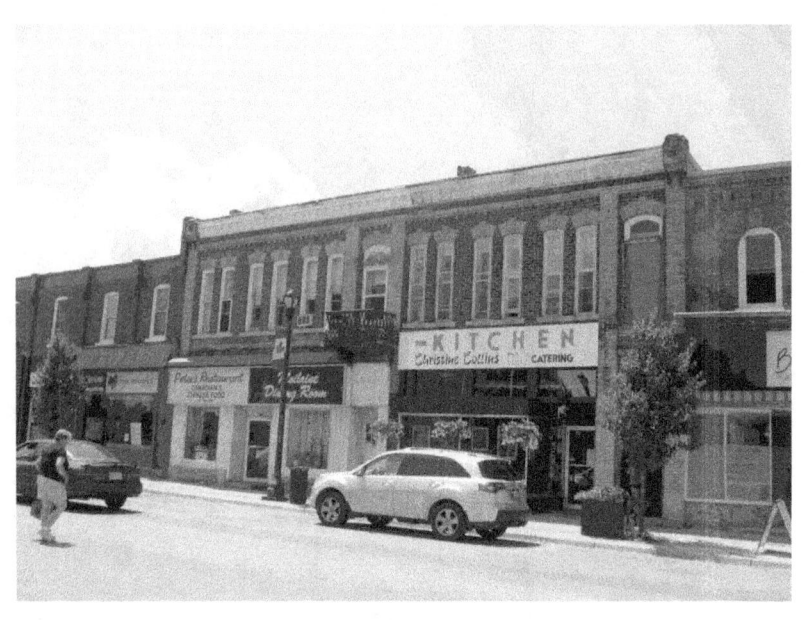

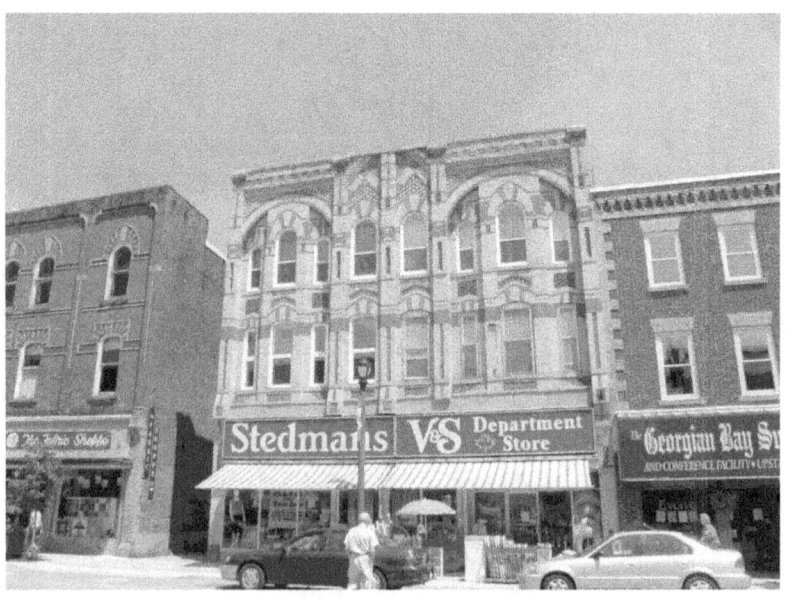

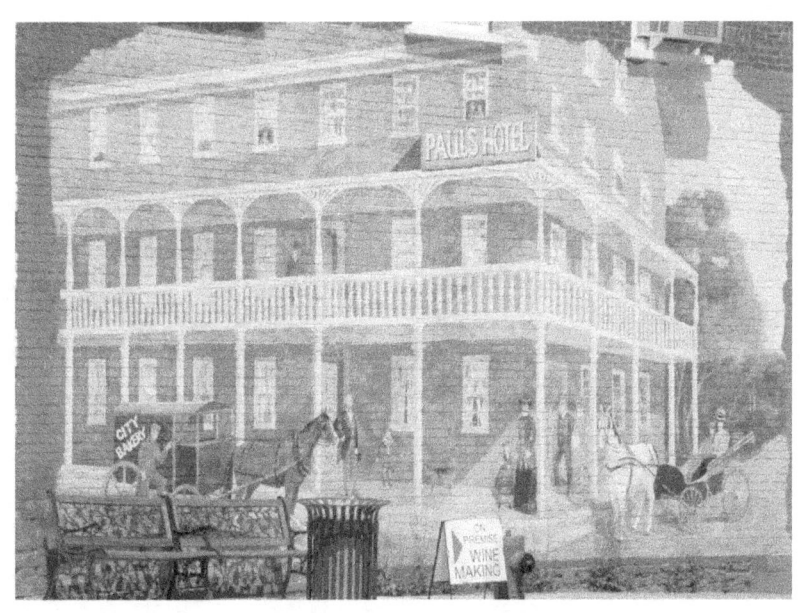

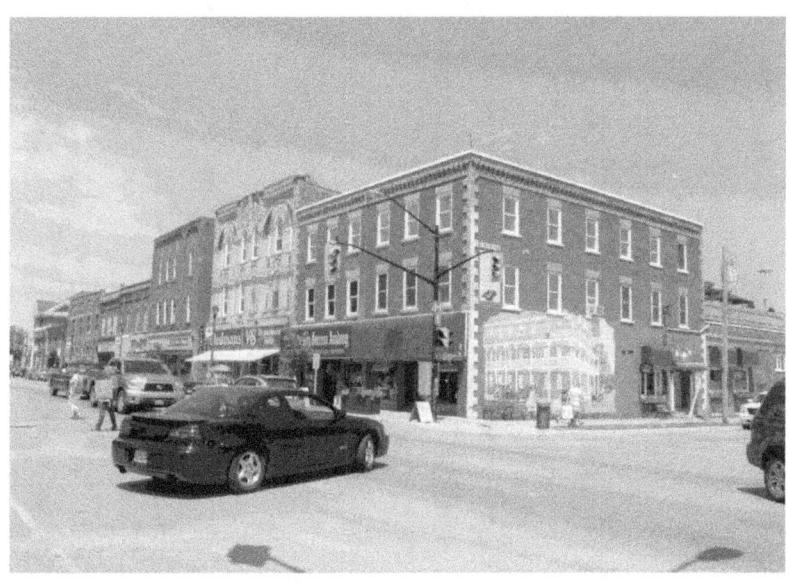

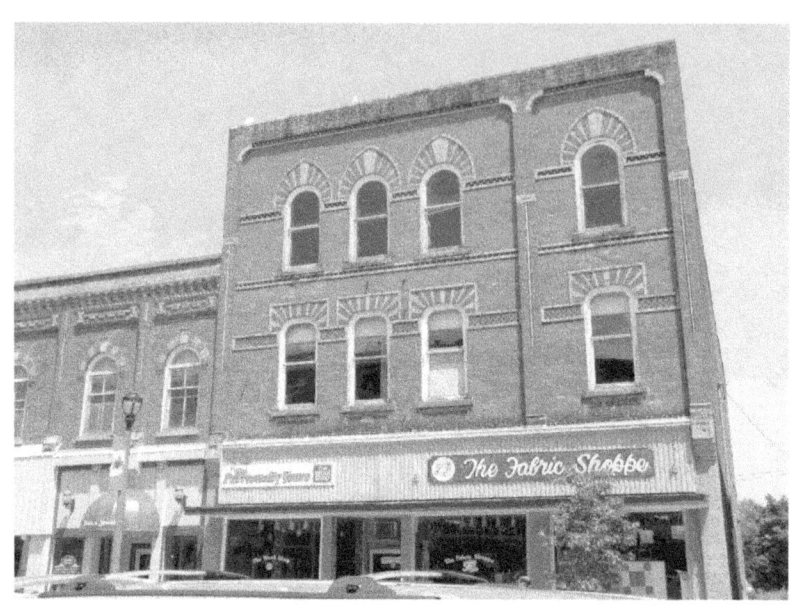

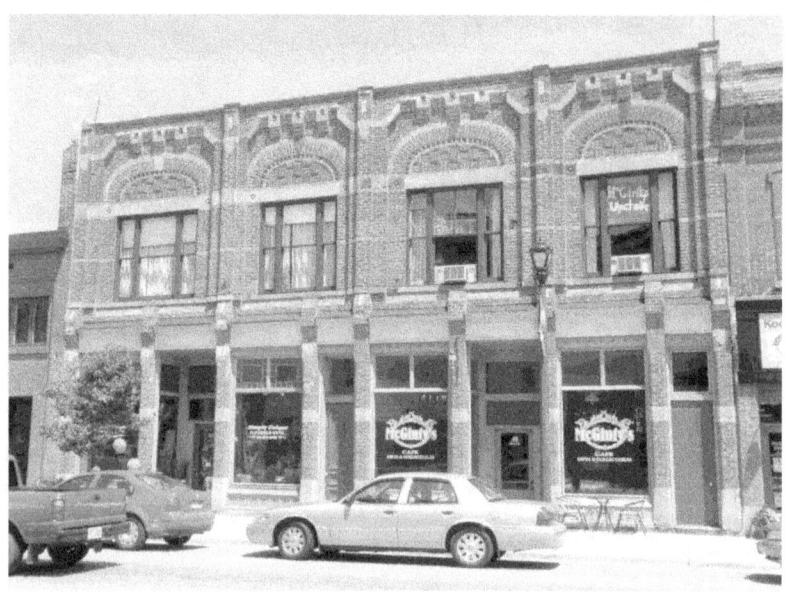

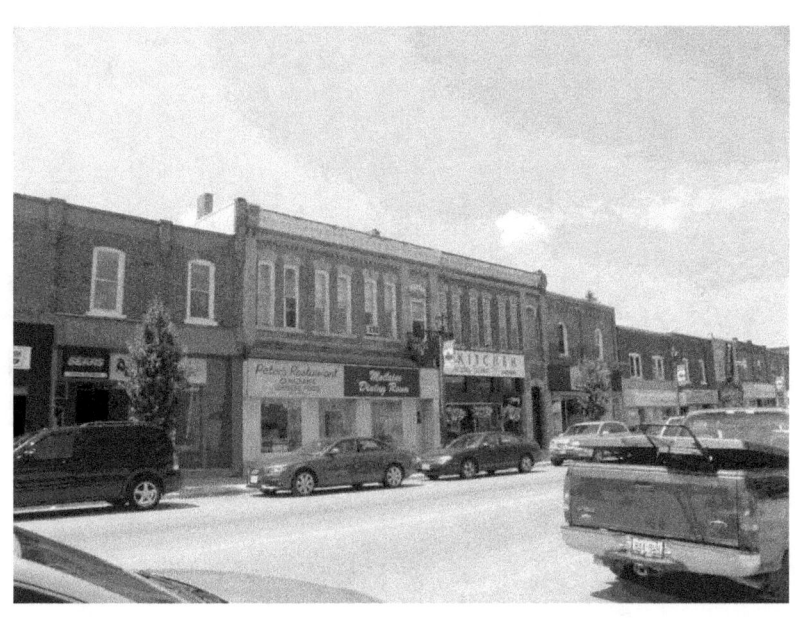

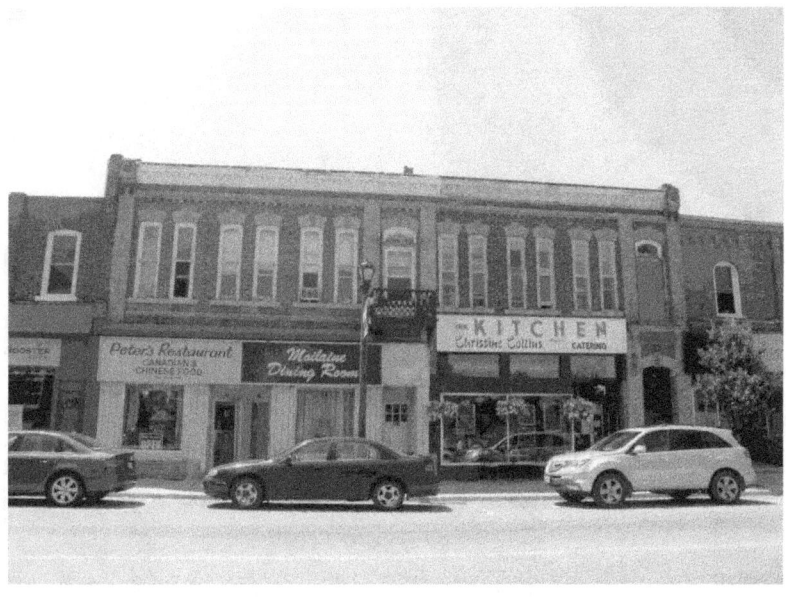

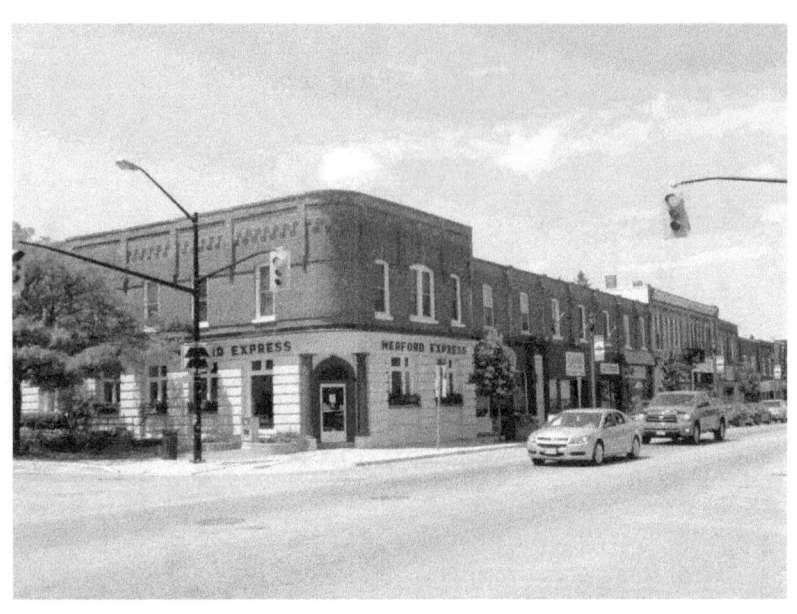

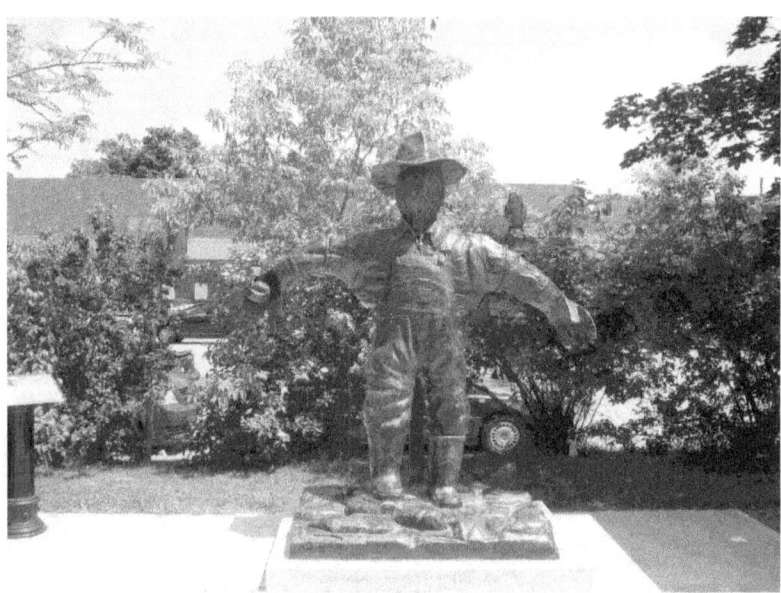

Schubird – Welcome to Meaford

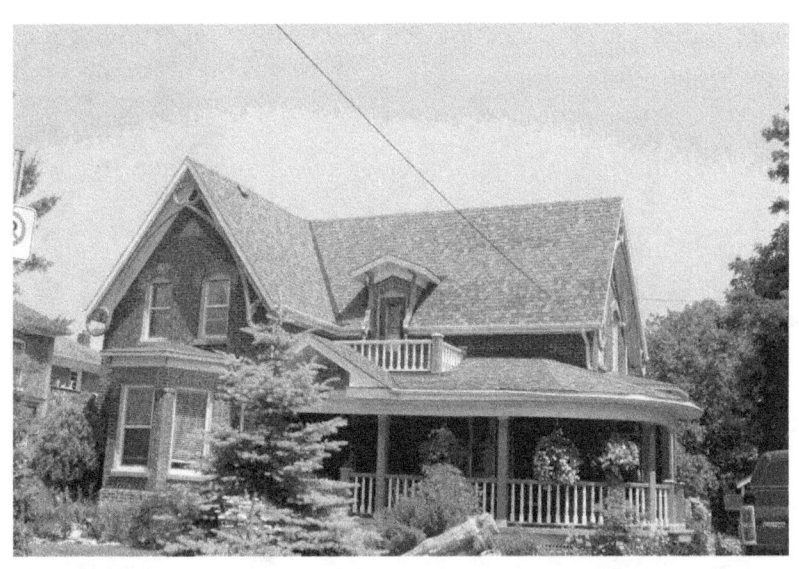

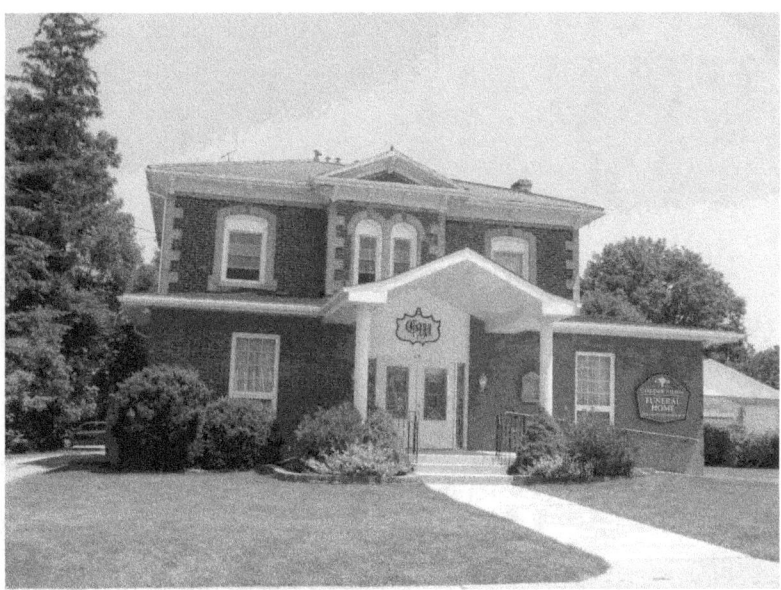

Gardiner-Wilson Funeral Home

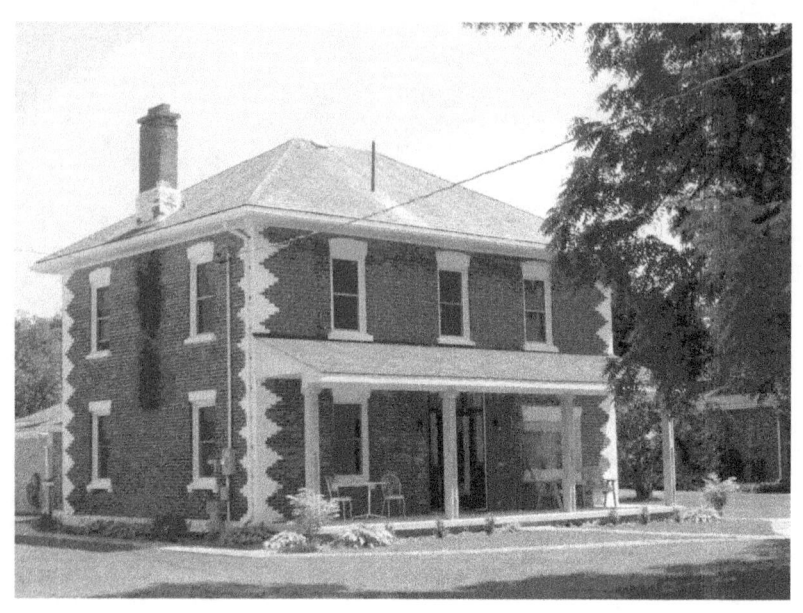

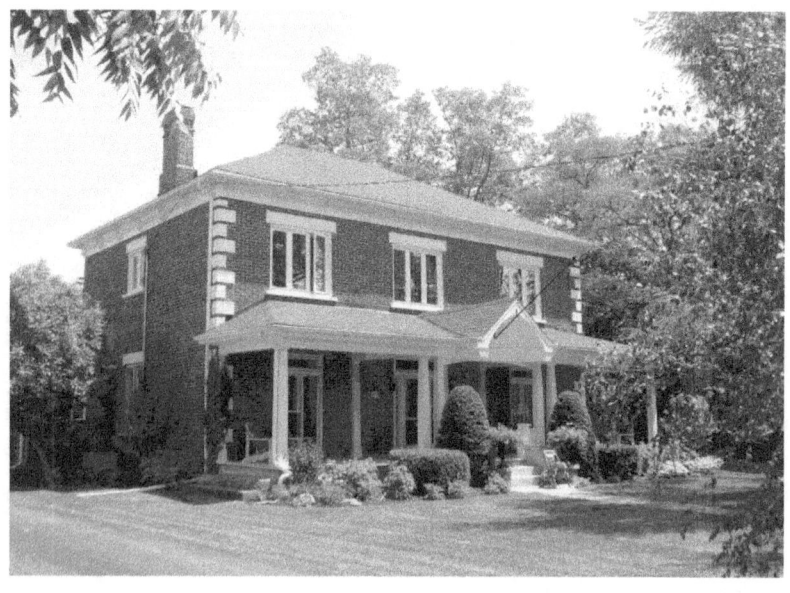

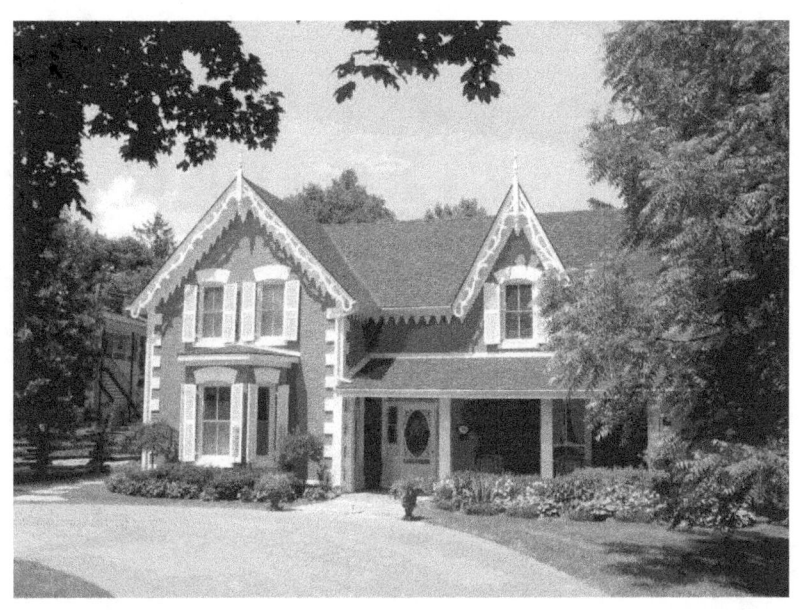

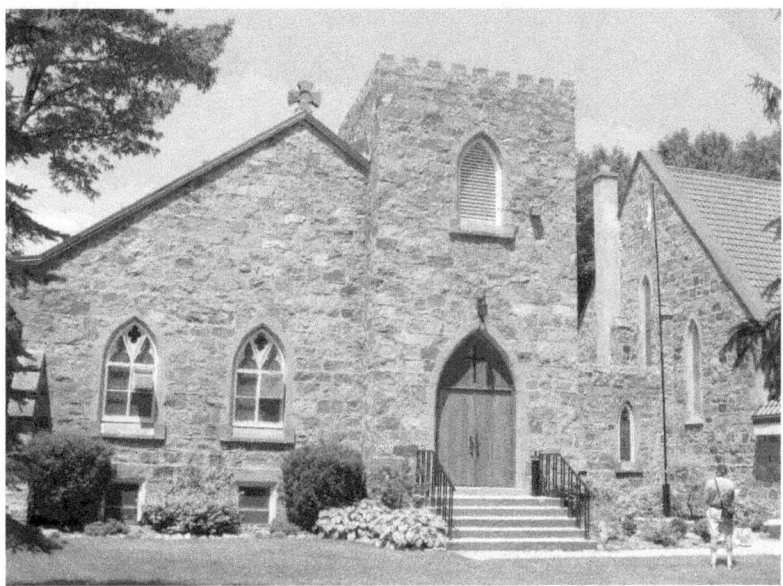

Christ Church Anglican

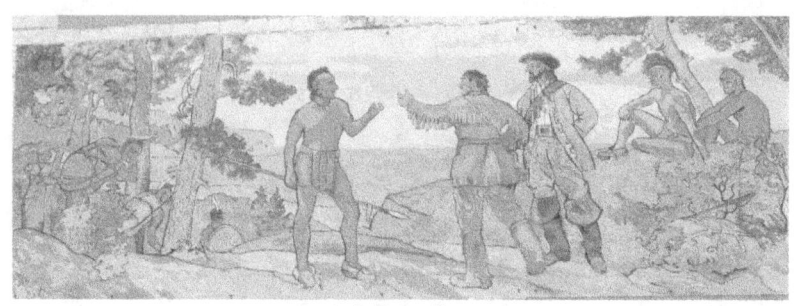

Mural

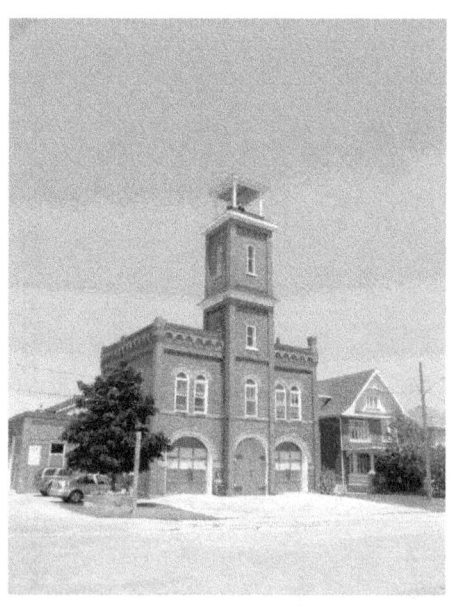

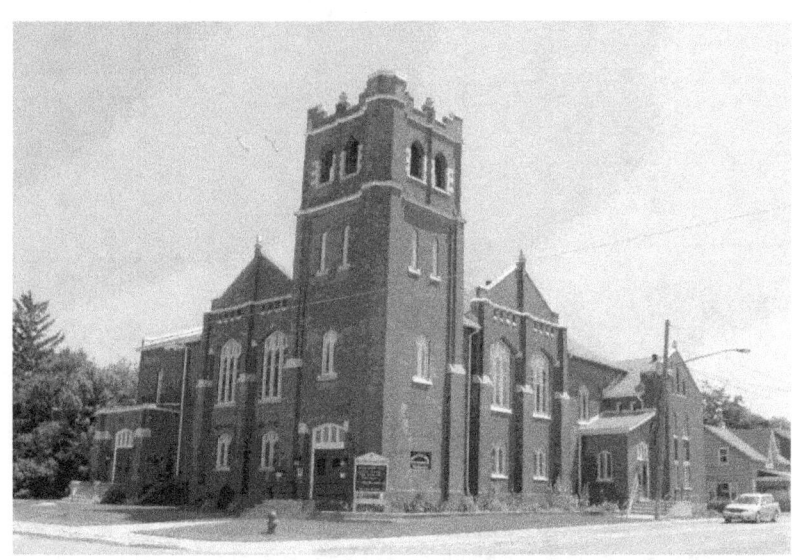

Meaford United Church

Thornbury

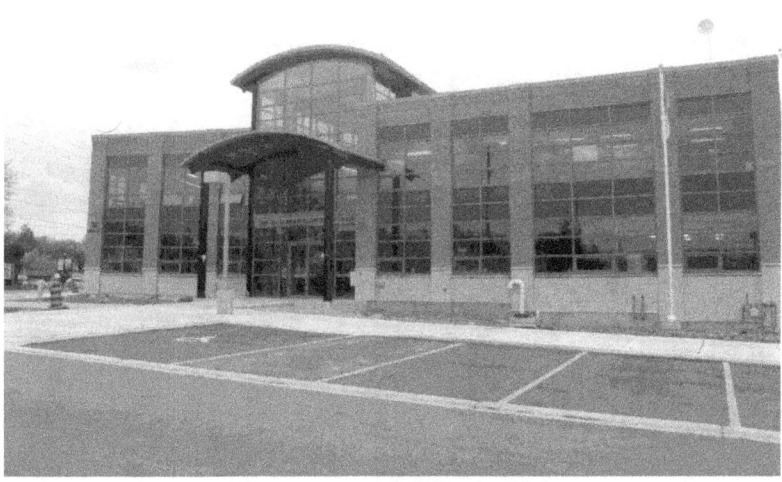

New City Hall building

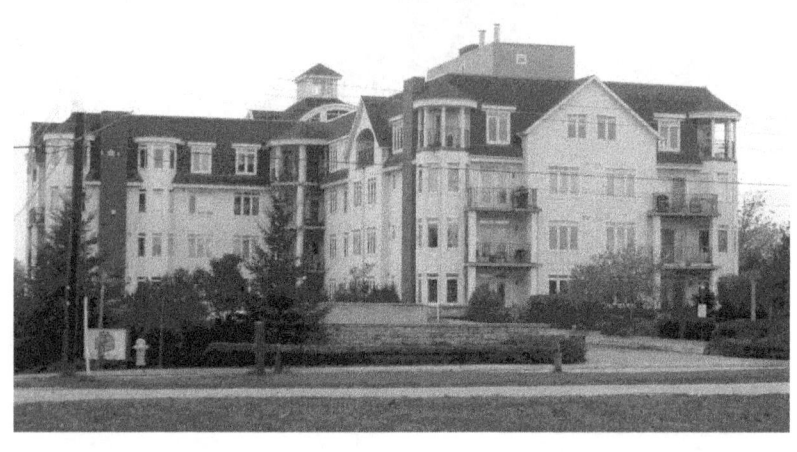

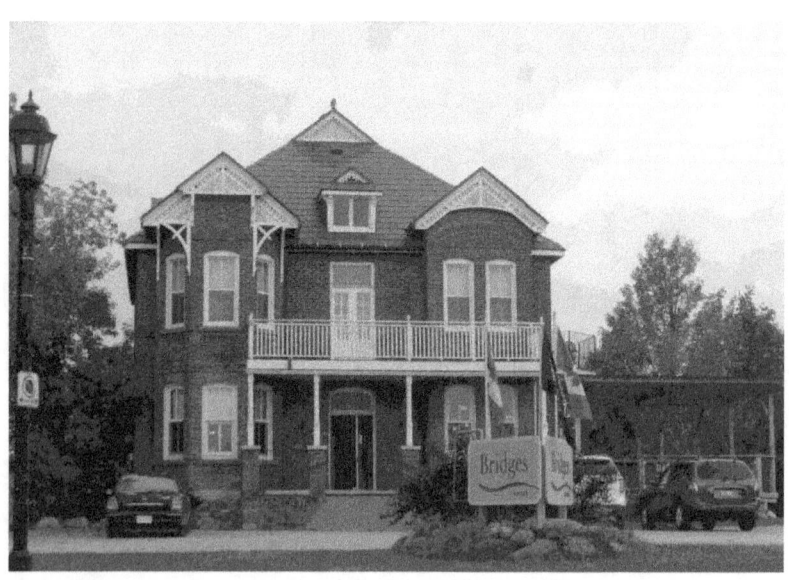

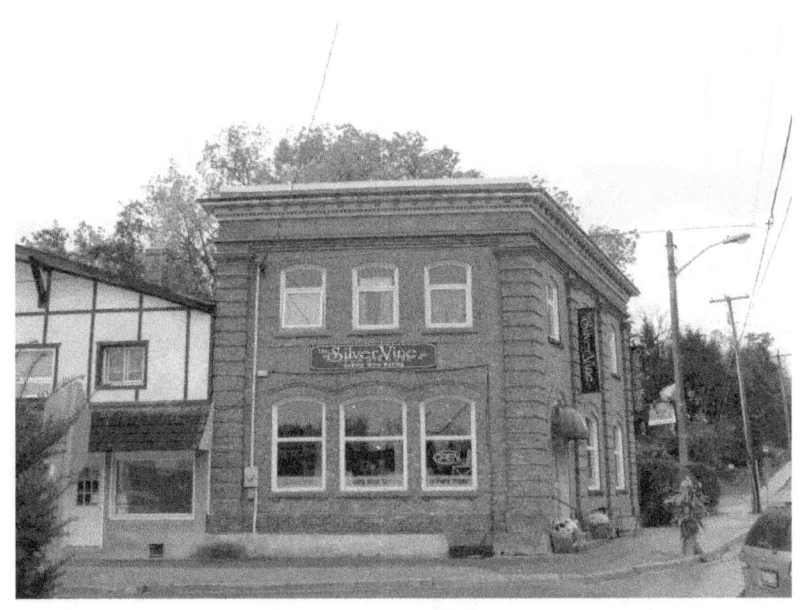

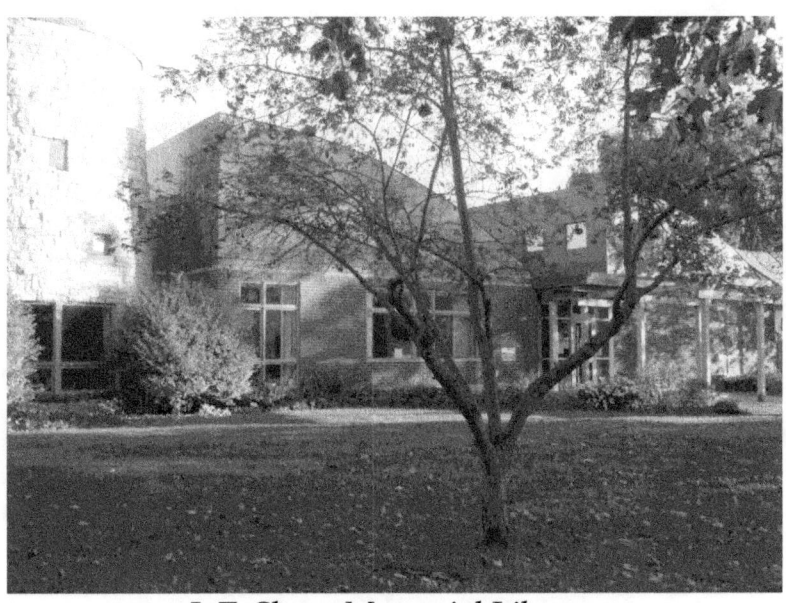

L.E. Shore Memorial Library

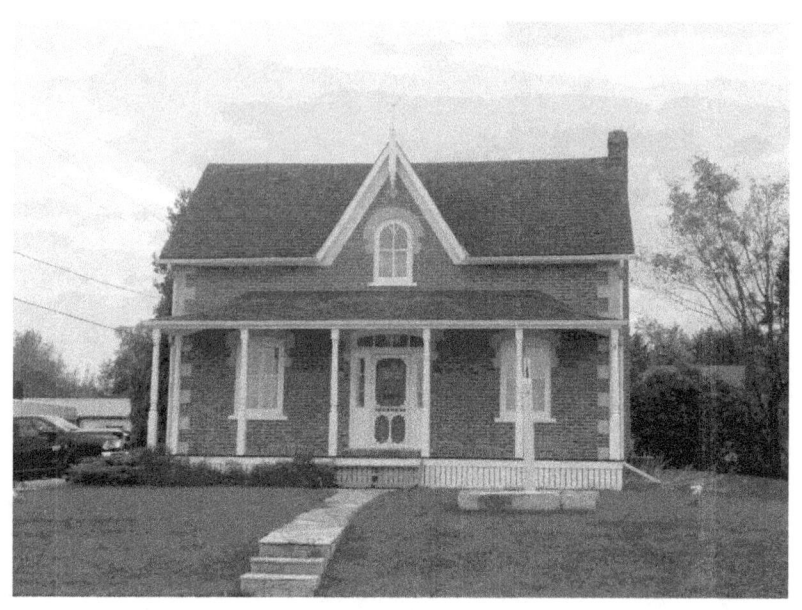

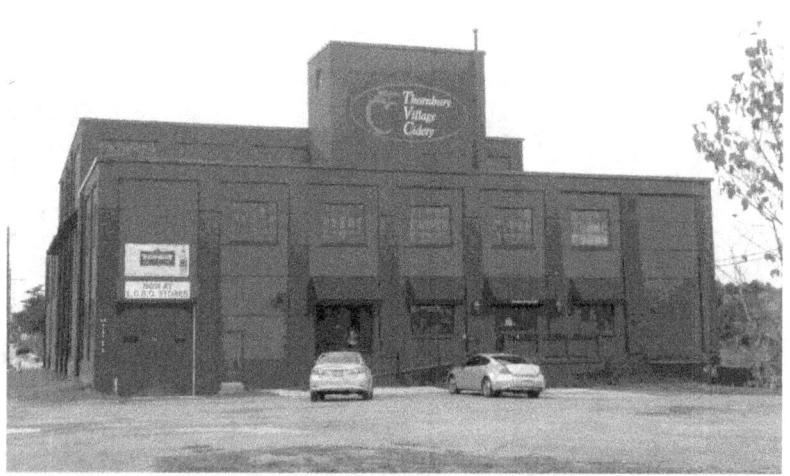

Thornbury Village Cidery

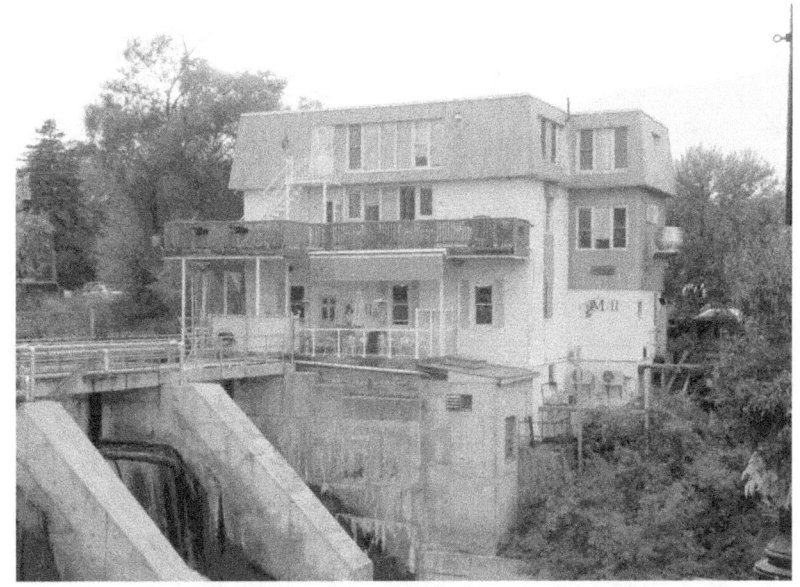

Dam by the old mill which is now a restaurant

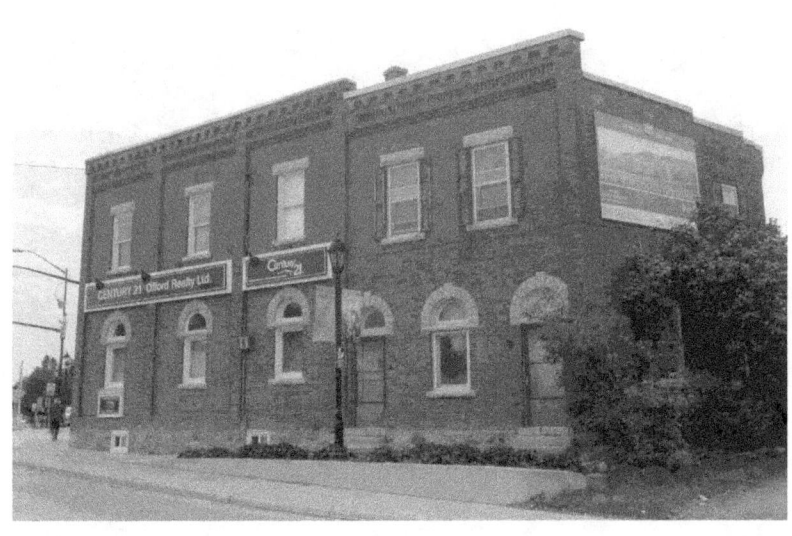

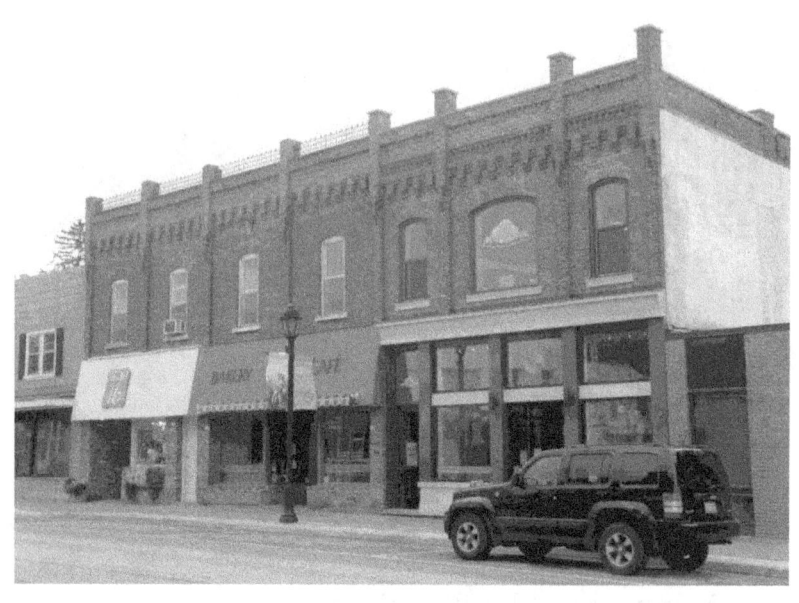

Downtown buildings

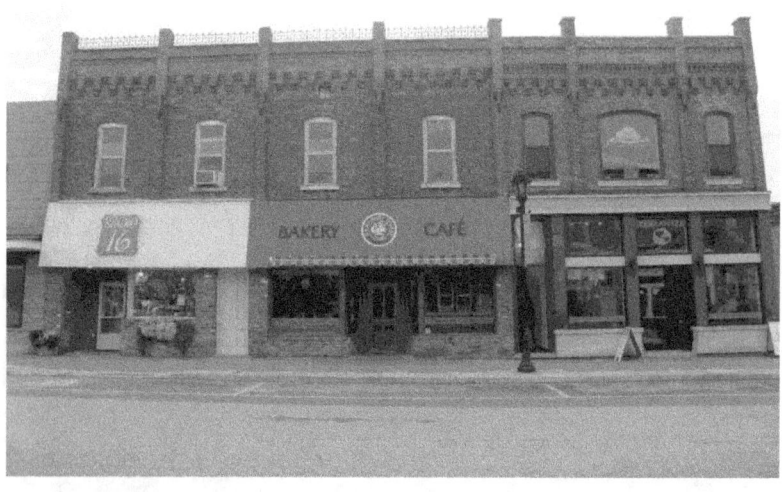

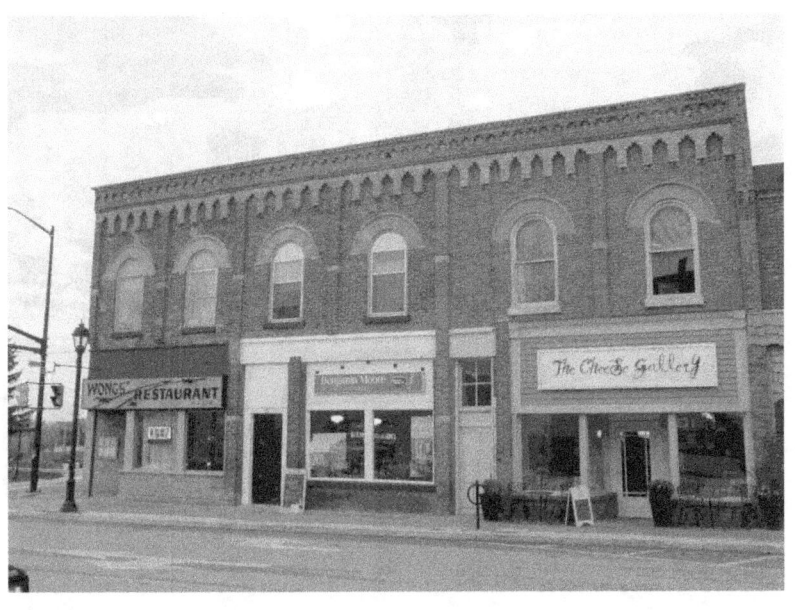

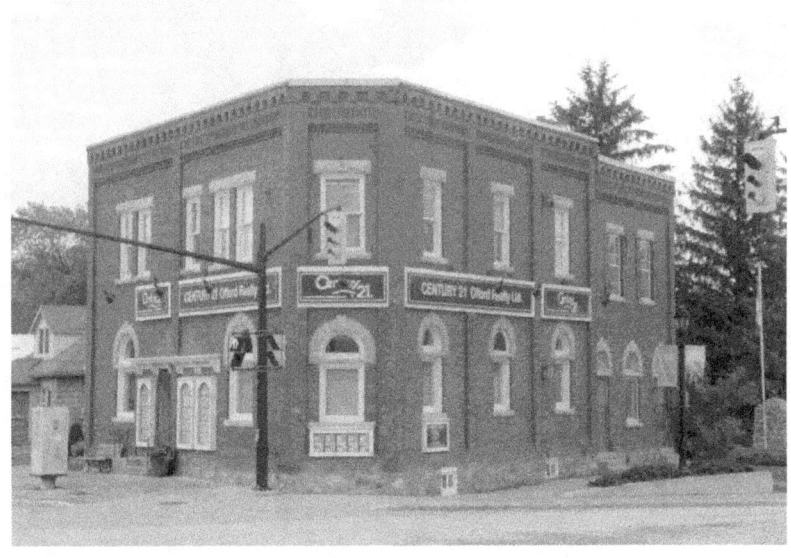

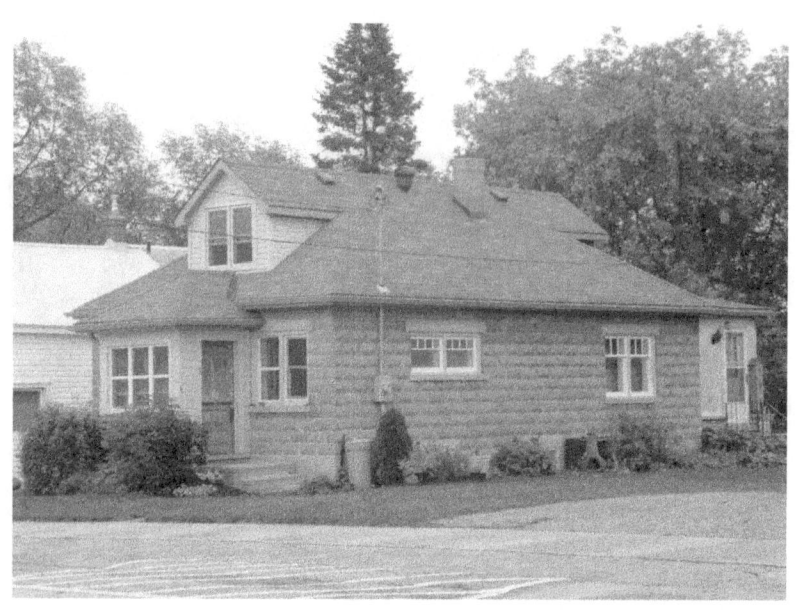

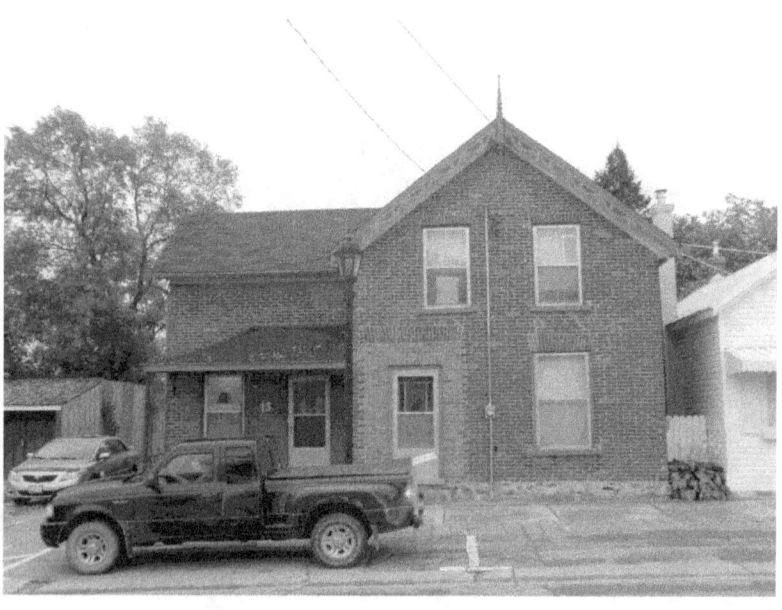

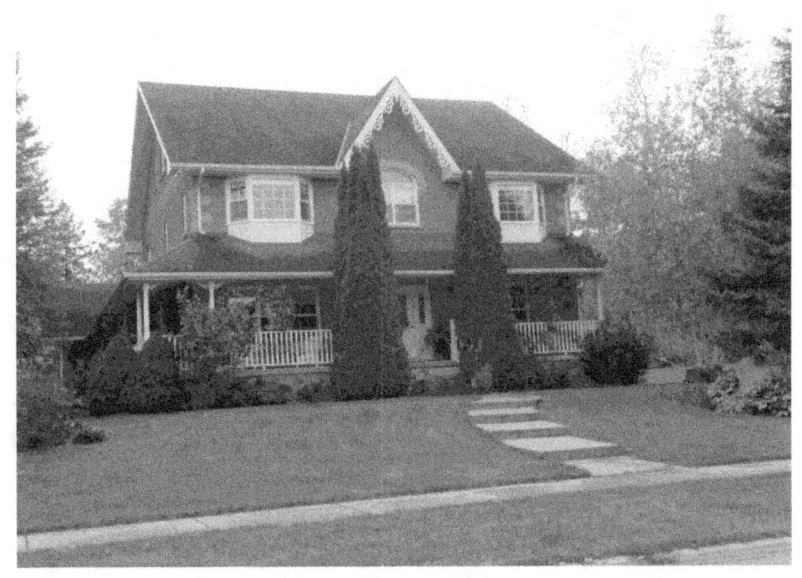

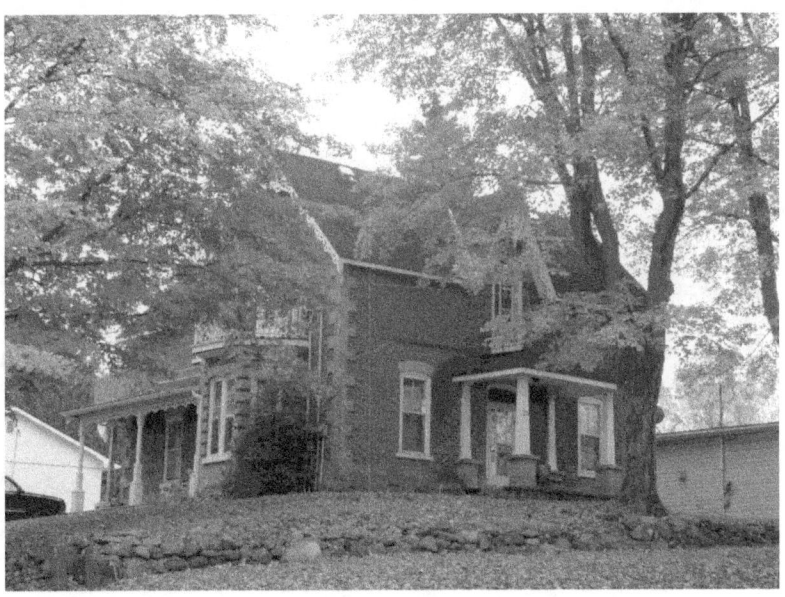

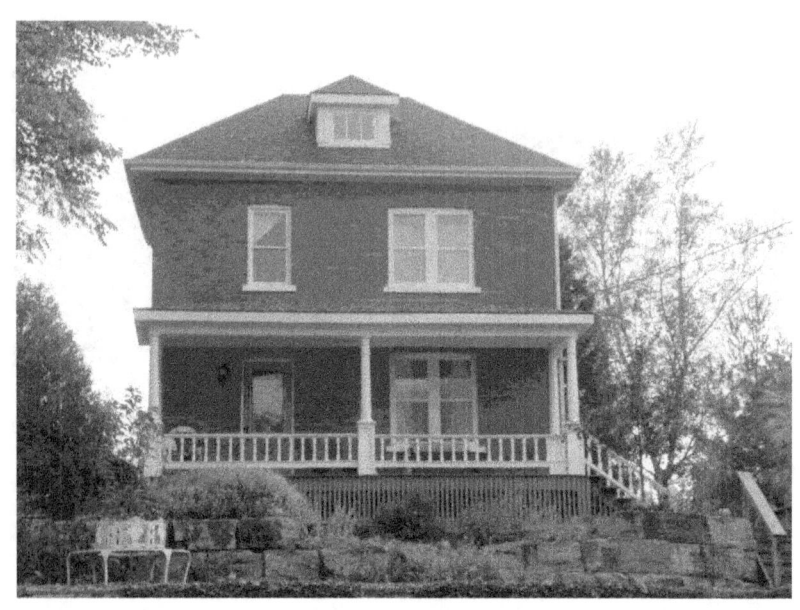

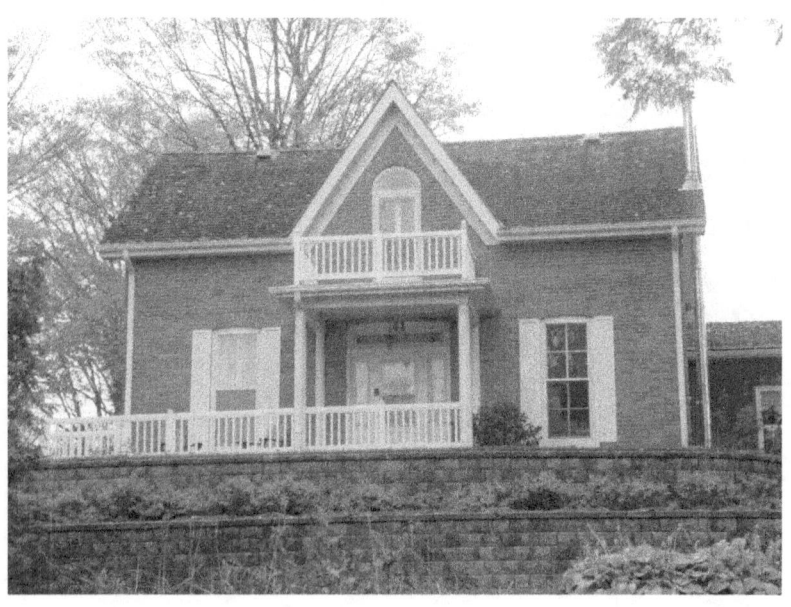

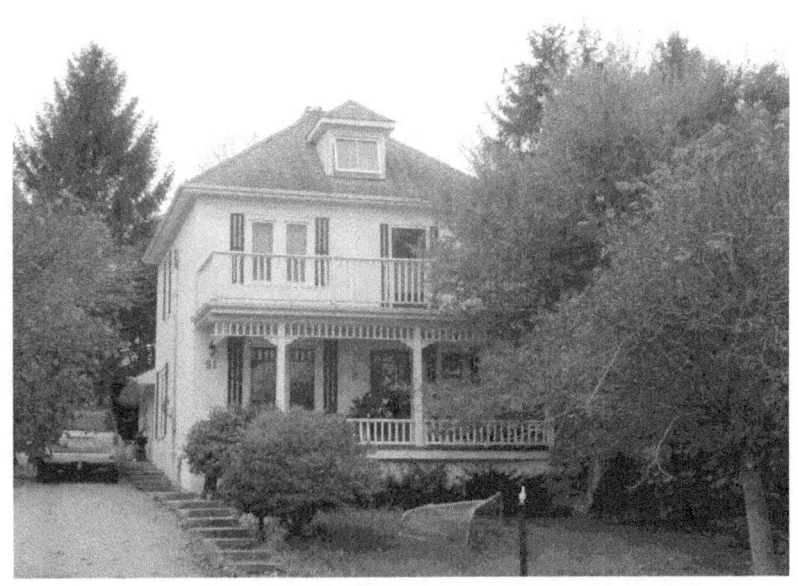

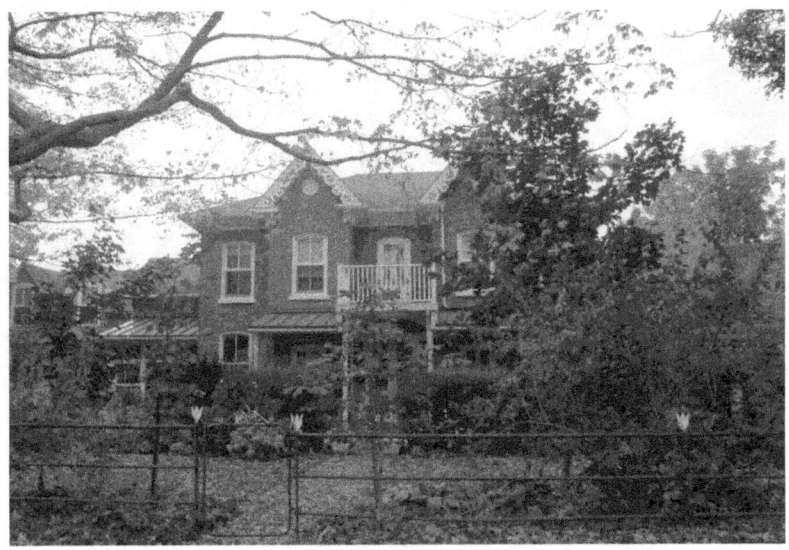

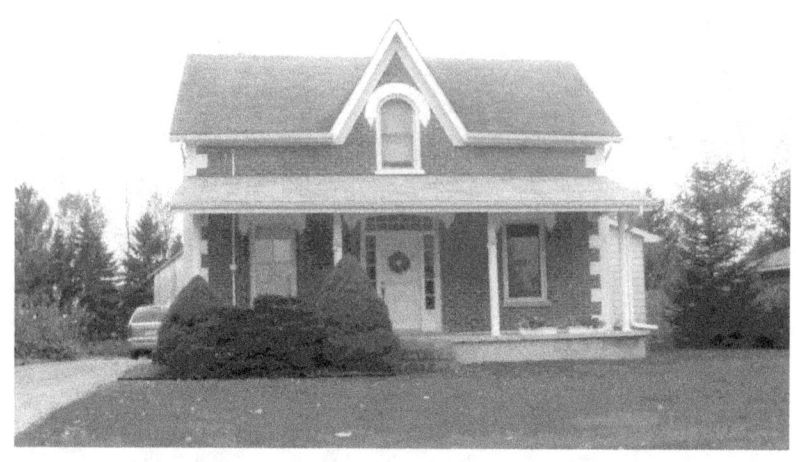

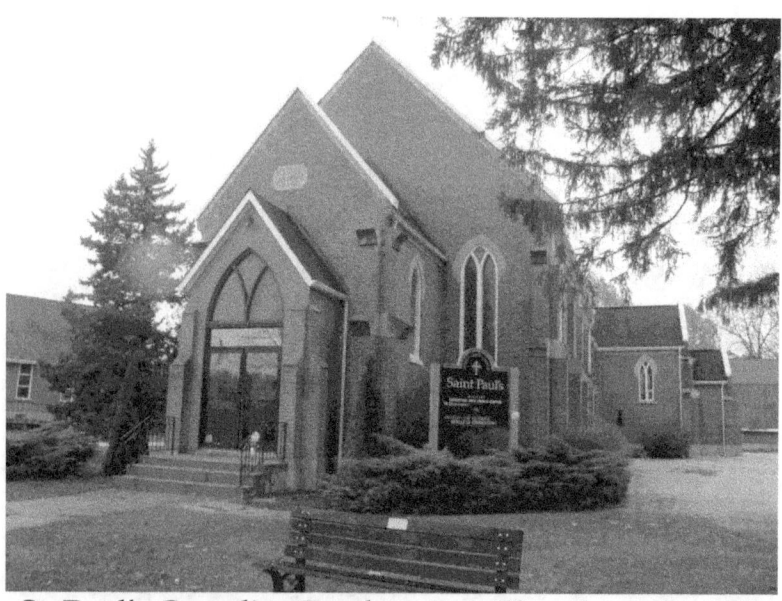

St. Paul's Canadian Presbyterian Church - A.D. 1880

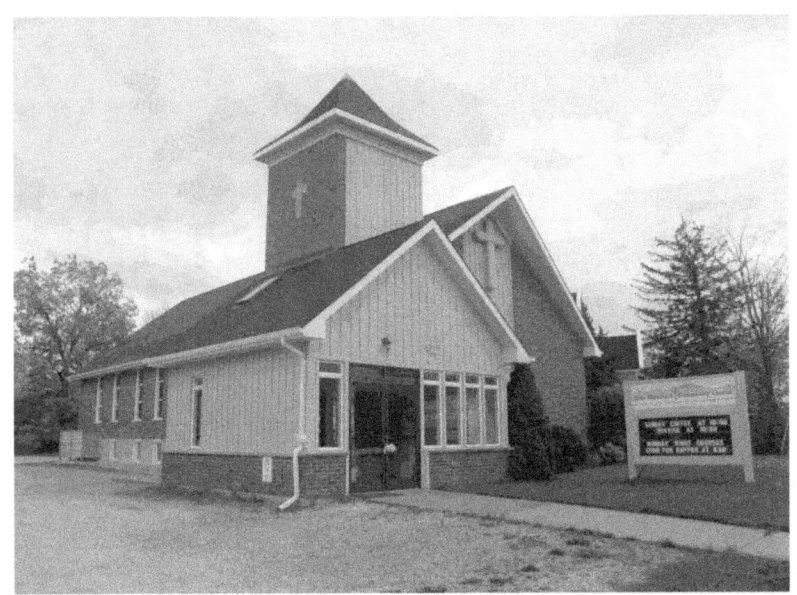

Blue Mountain Community Church

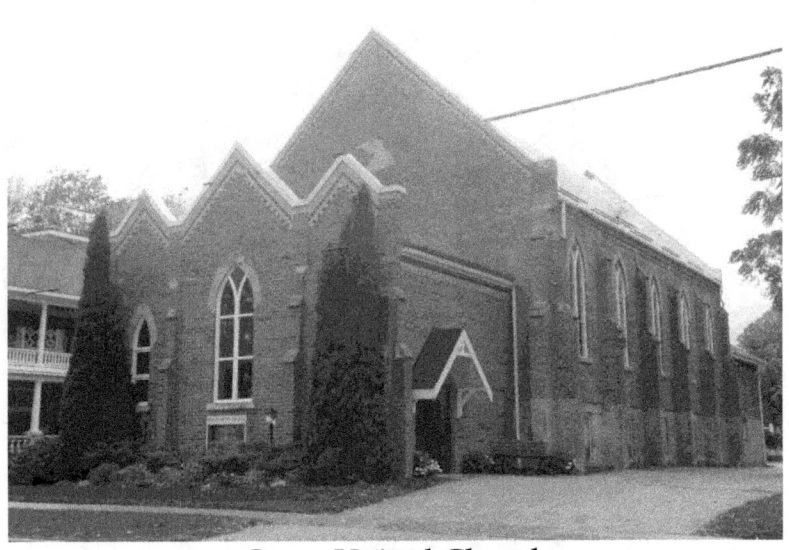

Grace United Church
Former Methodist Church of Canada 1880

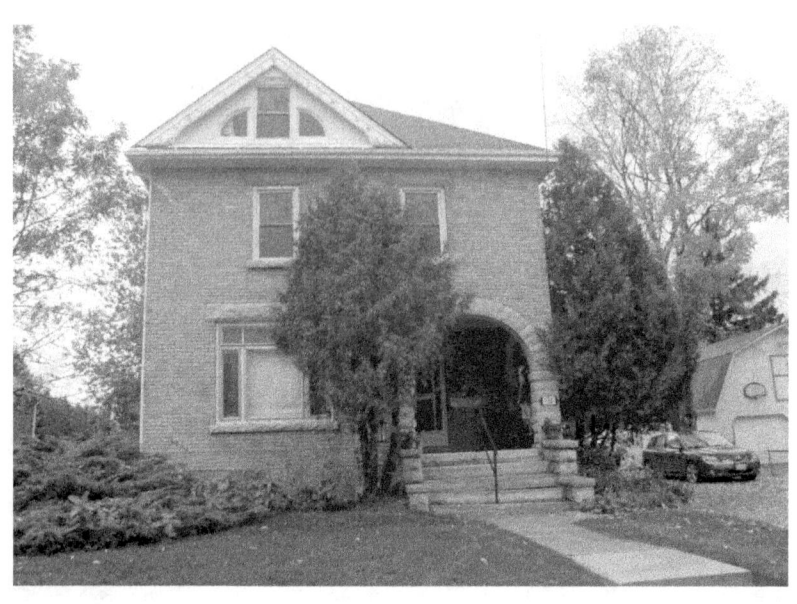

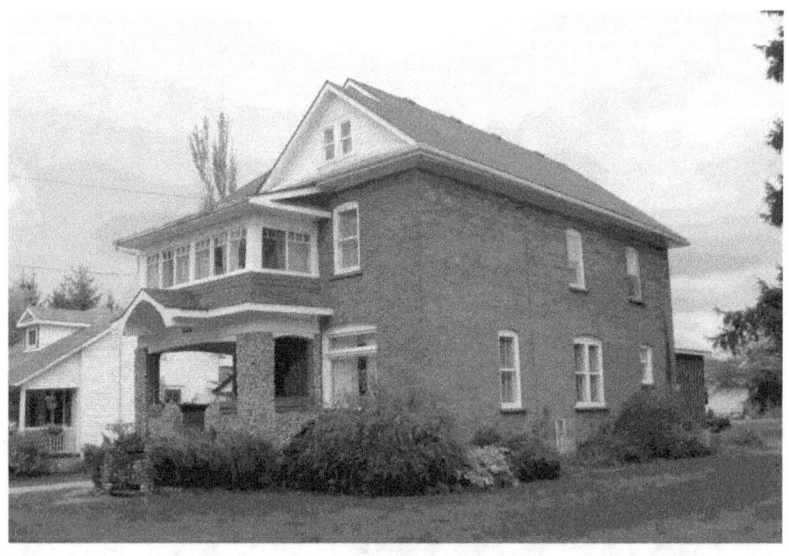

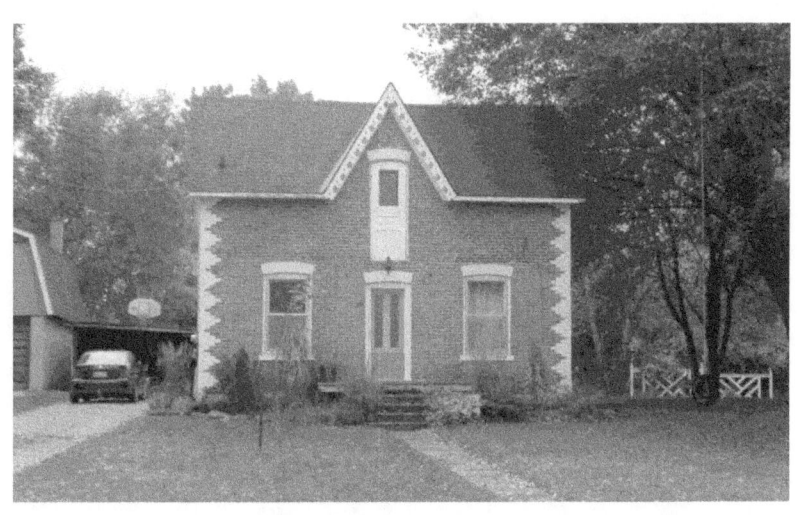

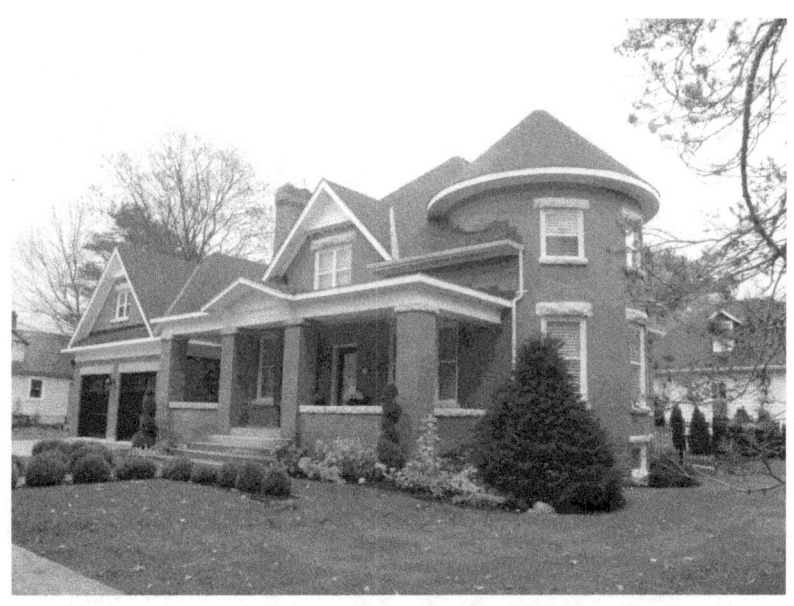

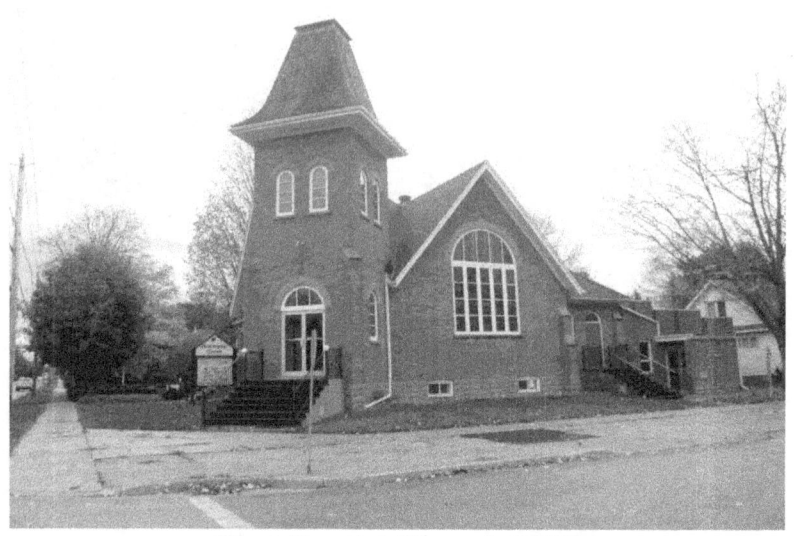

First Baptist Church 1907

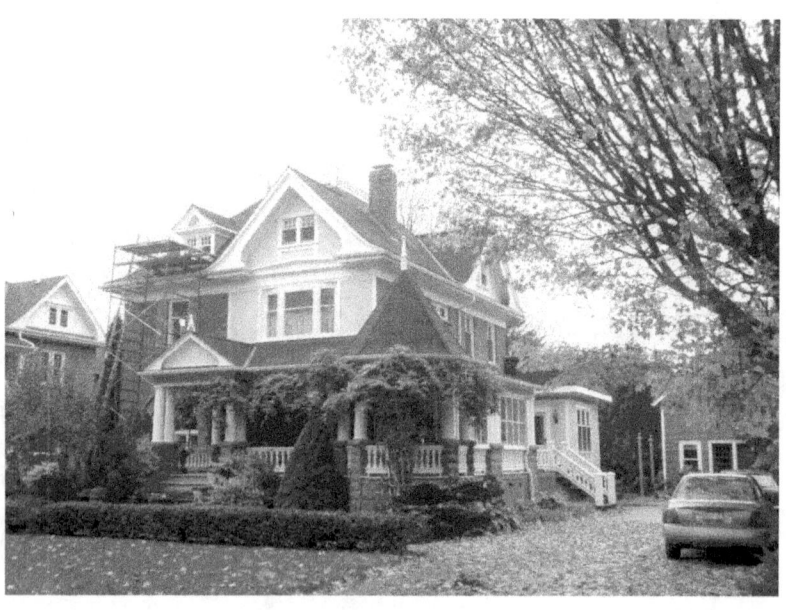

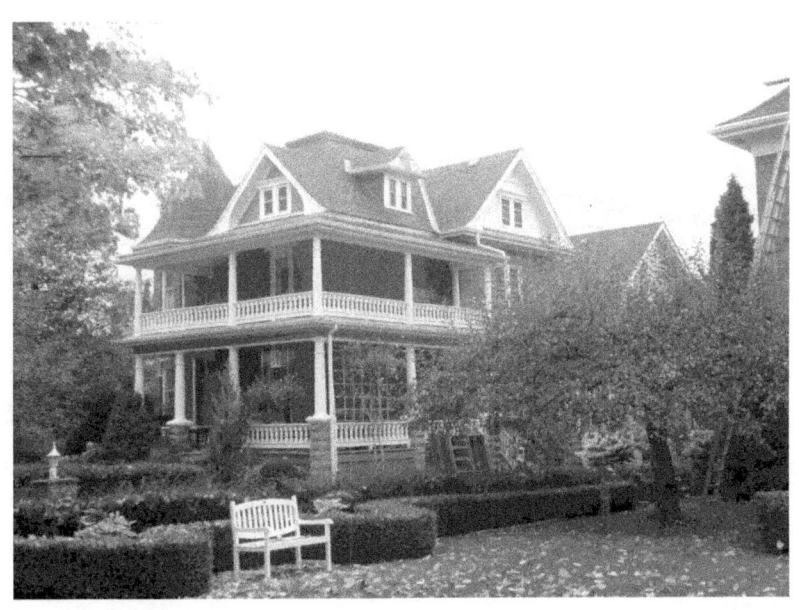

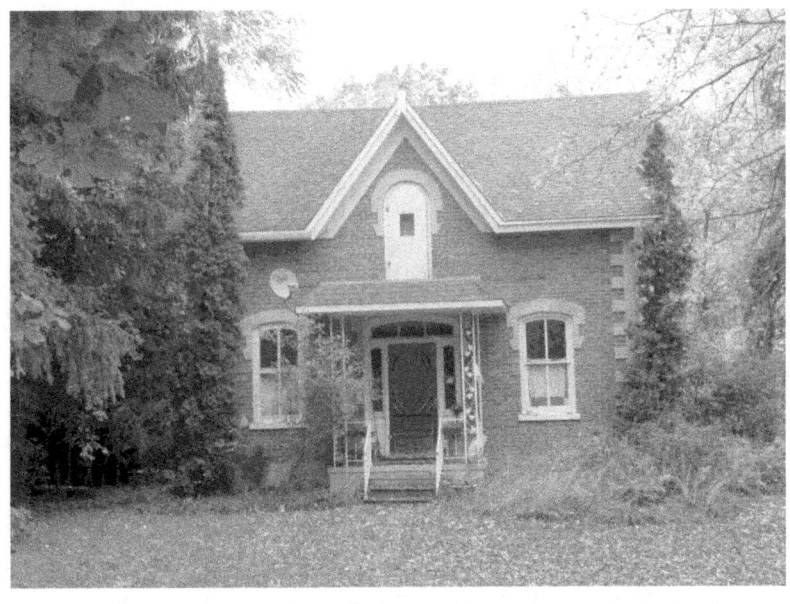

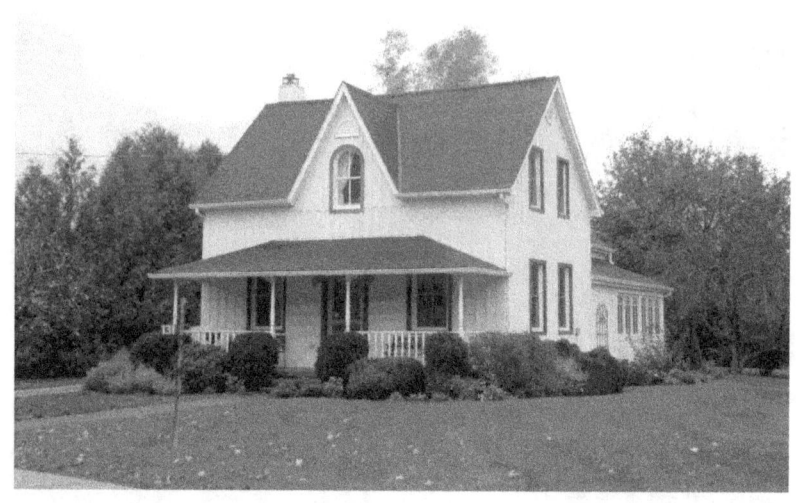

Victoria Corners

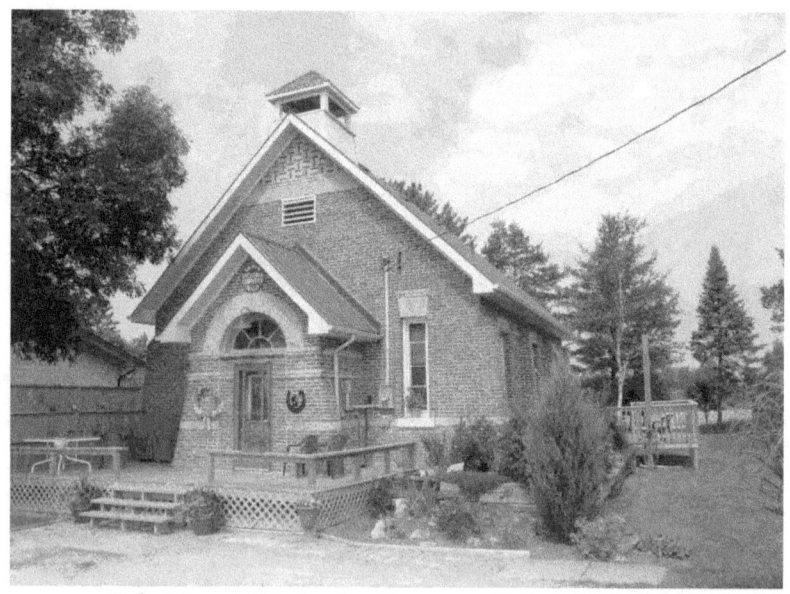

S.S. No. 4 Victoria Corners School – 1880

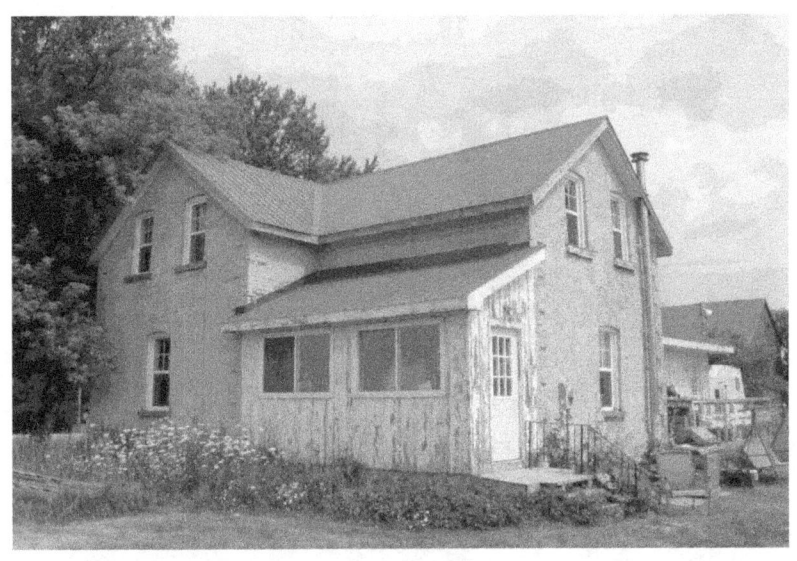

Walter's Falls

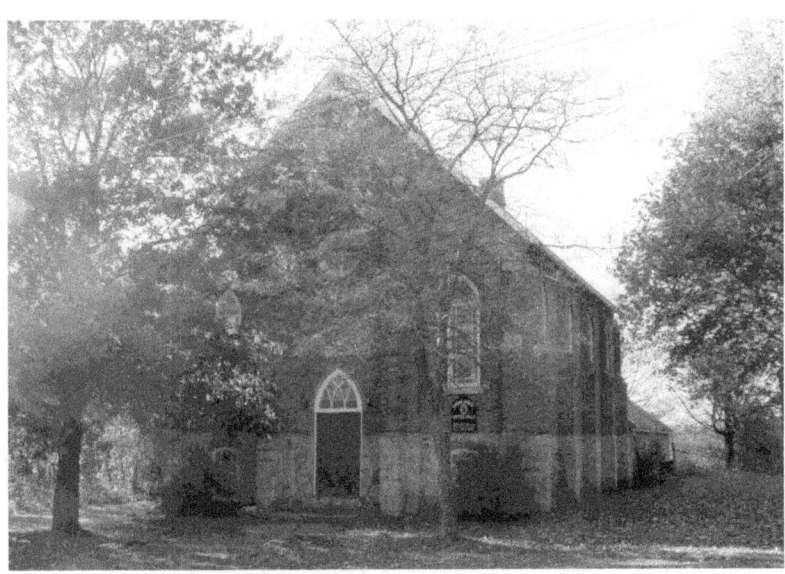

United Church – 167 Victoria Street

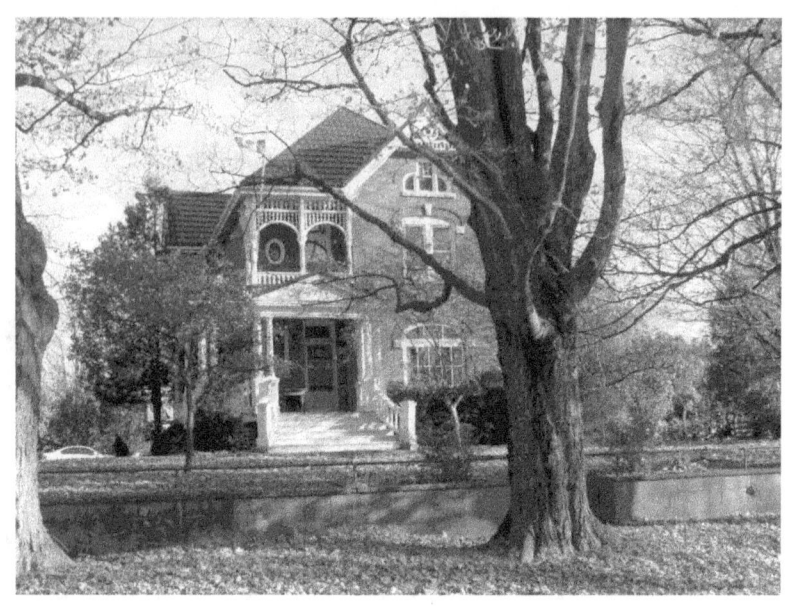

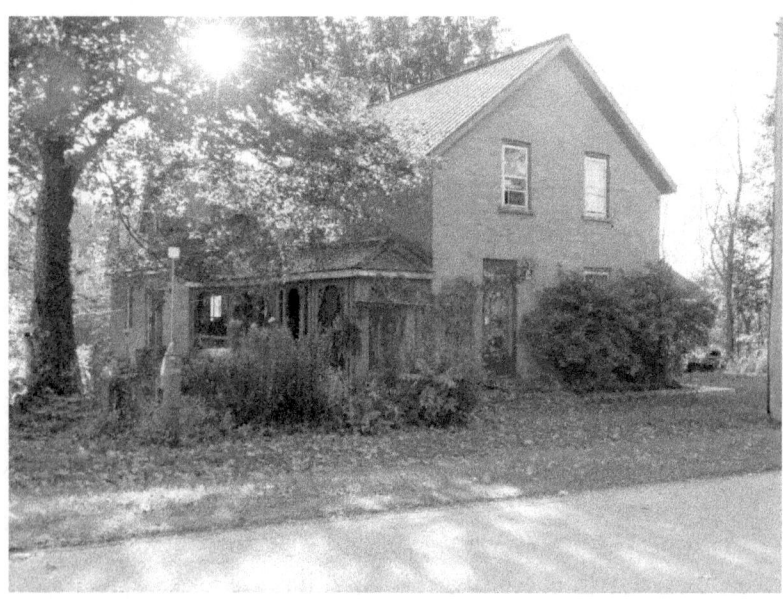

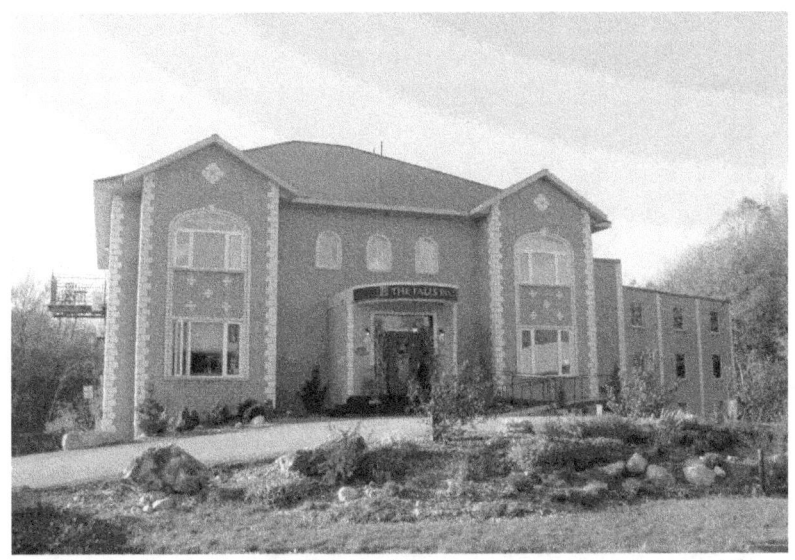

The Falls Inn and Spa – 14-room country inn with spa treatment rooms perched on top of Walter's Falls on the Bruce Trail

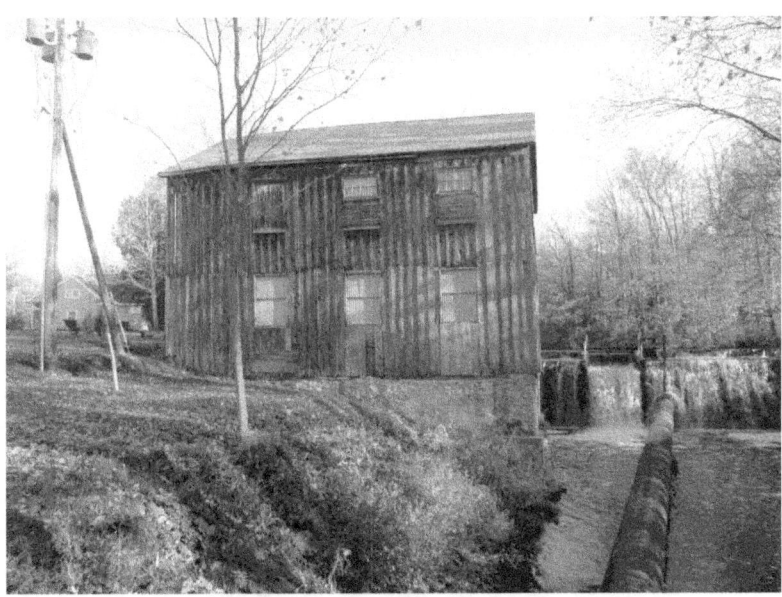

Old Woollen Mill by Walter's Falls

www.ingramcontent.com/pod-product-compliance
Lightning Source LLC
Chambersburg PA
CBHW071627170526
45166CB00003B/1222